Newly Revised Edition

Learning At Home:

A Mother's Guide
To Homeschooling

Marty Layne

Marty Layne

Sea Change Publications
Victoria, B.C.
Canada

Please note:

Before starting to homeschool, check with your provincial or state education department for regulations applying to homeschooling. These regulations vary from place to place. This book does not address the legal implications or requirements of homeschooling. The author assumes no responsibility for any action taken regarding homeschooling. Readers should find out what is legally required to homeschool in the area in which they live.

Newly Revised Edition
Learning At Home: A Mother's Guide to Homeschooling

Published by:
Sea Change Publications
1850 San Lorenzo Ave.
Victoria, B. C. V8N 2E9 Canada

10 09 08 07 06 05 04

Library and Archives Canada Cataloguing in Publication
Layne, Marty, 1948 -
Learning at home : a mother's guide to homeschooling / by Marty
Layne. -- Newly rev. ed.

Includes bibliographical references.
ISBN 978-0-9682938-4-3
1. Home schooling. I. Title.

LC40.L39 2007   371.04'2   C2007-900392-3

Dedicated to
my husband, Larry,
and our children, Josh, Noah, Robin, and Holly,
with love,
and in memoriam to
Henry C. Layne (1907 -1988)
and Maria Blomme (1919 - 2003)

Marty Layne provides coaching, workshops and seminars for those interested in learning more about homeschooling and parenting. Inquiries about her availability should be directed care of the publisher at the address below. The author welcomes comments and suggestions for future editions of this book.

To contact the author or order copies of this book contact:
Sea Change Publications
1850 San Lorenzo Ave.
Victoria, B.C. V8N 2E9
Canada   250-477-0173
www.martylayne.com
email: info@martylayne.com

A note about the various editions of this book:

I wrote the first edition of this book in response to the many requests for information about homeschooling that I received. It was written to inform, support, and encourage anyone considering homeschooling as well as to provide new ideas and directions, support, and encouragement for those who are already homeschooling.

The Revised Edition was released in 2000 and was a Crossings Book Club Selection in 2001. It was also translated into Indonesian and 2000 paperback copies of *Ibuku Guruku (My Mother, My Teacher)* were published in Sept., 2005 in Indonesia. The translator lives in the same town in Indonesia where my father was born. I only wish my father was still alive so that he could read the book to me.

CONTENTS

Photo credits:
Larry Layne Front cover and pages 156, 189, 201, 202
Marty Layne Pages 12, 16, 84, 87, 95, 96, 164, 180, 189, 217, 218, 220, 221, 222
Maria Blomme Page 25
Noah Layne Back cover

Cover design Noah Layne

INTRODUCTION

This book is written from a mother's point of view. I started writing this book in 1995. It took me three years to complete and publish the first edition. It took me three years to complete because I was writing in "mother time." My writing took place in odd times, in odd places, and in spurts. I enjoyed the whole process. Two years later, I published the revised edition. It included material new to the first edition. This newly revised edition issued nine years after the first edition also incorporates new material and a different perspective now that my youngest child is 21 years old.

Mothering and homeschooling gave me a chance to develop myself in ways that I could never have imagined before I started. In Western culture, freedom from child caring responsibilities is often seen as the best and only way for a mother to continue to develop herself. I couldn't disagree more. The time I spent being at home, playing and learning with my children, has been the most productive period of my life.

My experience as a homeschooling mother helped me to appreciate the importance of relationships and to value the interdependence of children and their mothers. At a time when we in the Western world are lurching along trying to reconcile our way of life with the ecological effects it has on the whole planet, an opportunity to explore the issue of interdependence in rearing children may seem irrelevant. However, until we treat all children with the care, love, and respect that is their birth right, we cannot learn to treat the earth that way.

My decision in my early twenties to move to a farm in Cape Breton, Nova Scotia was a move toward ecologically sound living practices. It was also an attempt to become independent. The five years I spent attempting to live as a self-sufficient farmer showed me how impossible it is to live independently. We need so many things we cannot provide for ourselves - everything from metals that are dug and smelted to communication tools. Independence as a goal is simplistic and impossible. Because of that experience, I approached motherhood with an appreciation of interdependence which was invaluable in raising my children.

As you will read about in the following chapters, this book is not intended to convince anyone that homeschooling is the only way of educating children. It is as much about establishing good relationships with children as about educating them. Therefore, it can be read by any mother, regardless of her choice of education for her children, and be helpful. Fathers, too, will find it informative.

If you are curious about homeschooling and wonder if it is something you could do, read on.

If you have a friend, relative, or neighbor who is homeschooling, this book can give you some insight as to why someone would choose this method of education.

If you are a teacher, you might find the idea of homeschooling uncomfortable. I hope that this book can help you to see that when someone chooses to homeschool, it is not a condemnation of the teaching profession. Instead, homeschooling parents can be seen as a source of ideas and insights about how children learn for we have the opportunity to work one on one with children that few teachers have.

If you are a parent who is pleased with the way school is working for your family and are interested in providing learning opportunities for your child in your home, this book can give you some ideas to use to supplement your child's schooling.

My husband, Larry, and I have four children, Josh born in 1977, Noah born in 1979, Robin born in 1982, and Holly born in 1985. They learned at home from birth through grade 12.

This book is a compilation of actual experiences in helping my children learn at home, methods I borrowed from others, my thoughts and observations of the learning process, and reflections now that my children are all adults. It is meant as a guide to give you an idea of what homeschooling might be like. It is not meant as the definition of how all homeschooling should be done.

Homeschooling has proved to be successful for many. However, like any method of educating children, there are no guarantees. We can never know the outcome before we start. Each child brings a different gift to this planet Earth. Homeschooling will not make a child become a musical genius or a computer whiz. No method of education can turn a tulip into a daffodil. However, homeschooling can help you to nurture your children so that they will grow to be themselves. And as a side benefit, homeschooling can also help you become more aware of your own gifts and talents.

Robin, Josh, Holly, Noah

Teaching can only happen when there is someone willing to be the learner as well as someone willing to be the teacher.

CHAPTER 1
Can I Do This -
Teach My Child At Home?

The characteristics it takes to homeschool
How to acquire those characteristics

B efore I list the characteristics which I think are important in order to be able to teach your child at home, let me define what I mean by teaching. *The New Lexicon Webster's Encyclopedic Dictionary of the English Language, Canadian Edition* lists four definitions for teach, three of which I quote "to give instruction to, to train; to give to another knowledge or skill which one has oneself; to cause to understand." With this as a basis, I extend this definition to also mean being aware of when the child is ready to receive the teaching. In other words, just because I am ready to give my child instruction in reading doesn't mean my child is ready or able to receive it.

When I taught, I tried to be aware of my child's ability, readiness, and desire to learn a particular subject; to be sensitive to my child's motivation; and to be aware of my own motivation in wanting to teach a particular something to my child. Teaching can only happen when there is someone willing to be the learner as well as someone willing to be the teacher. The method used to instruct needs to be suitable to the person receiving the instruction.

With this definition of teaching in mind, I have drawn up a list of characteristics that I think are important to have in order to succeed at teaching your child at home. As you read through the list keep in mind that the first characteristic is something that you must have to start with, the others can be acquired and developed over time.

To succeed at homeschooling you need to:

1. Genuinely like your child or children and enjoy his, her, or their company
2. Have a sense of humor
3. Be able to read, write and do basic math and be willing to upgrade your skills as necessary
4. Have a commitment to a philosophy that leads you to homeschool
5. Be willing to develop communication/listening skills
6. Be prepared to receive criticism for your decision to homeschool
7. Have a support system or network and/or a supportive partner
8. Be able to learn from mistakes
9. Be willing to develop limit setting skills
10. Be willing to develop patience
11. Be willing to develop observational skills
12. Be willing to change

1. Genuinely like your child or children and enjoy his, her, or their company

Although it may seem rather obvious, this characteristic is some times overlooked. I think it's the most important one. What does it mean to like your child? It means that you enjoy being with your child. You take delight in her presence. You enjoy listening to her tell you things, you enjoy observing how she learns new skills, you are pleased to be in relationship with your child. This may seem simplistic, but it's so important.

If your child is going to spend most of her waking hours in your company, it's vital to her well being that you enjoy the daily interactions between you. This doesn't mean that there won't be moments when you need peace and quiet and some time to yourself. However, if you are frequently resentful of your child's need for you and you are constantly irritated by your children's presence, homeschooling your children will not work for you.

Being with children all the time is not easy. Children's needs can bring up all sorts of unresolved personal problems for their parents. The more willing you are as an adult to face your own personal issues and own them, the more able you are to be in relationship with your child as he or she is rather than as you imagine he or she should be.

I worked with many children before having my own. I couldn't imagine before having children, how much I would love my own children. I loved watching them as they learned new things as babies and toddlers. I enjoyed their creativity and inventiveness and was fascinated by the way they learned things. Observing my children as they gained mastery of many skills led me to think and learn more about learning myself.

If you have enjoyed being home with your preschool children, and the thought of sending your 5 year old off to kindergarten makes you sad, you are someone who could homeschool. If you are a mom who has sent her children to school, spends a lot of time in the local elementary school helping in your children's classes, and are beginning to wonder why you're spending so much time with other people's children, you might be a likely candidate for homeschooling.

Stating that you need to like your children in order to succeed at homeschooling does not imply that someone who sends a child to school does not like her child. It also does not imply that you must find your child delightful to be with every moment of everyday. What I am saying is that when you homeschool, you will be in your child's company for many hours everyday. If you don't fundamentally enjoy your child's company, don't attempt to homeschool.

2. Have a sense of humor

Without a sense of humor being a mother can be a pretty grim business. As a homeschooling mother, humor is even more important. There are days when life with young children just seems more than any one person can cope with. No matter how hard one tries, the more confused everything gets. Life with children around all the time can be stressful and/or hilarious. It depends on your point of view. Laughter, like a breath 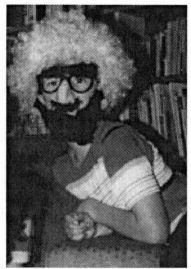 of fresh air, can clear away the frustrations of living with young children.

Being able to laugh and see the humor in many situations helped me to deal with the complications and "busy-ness" of life with four children. We played games like Charades or Mad Libs that sometimes left us all laughing so hard we cried. We read books that made us laugh. As everyone grew older, jokes gained popularity. Our humor was a gentle and positive kind, no sarcastic humor or teasing, just fun. Now that everyone is grown up, our all too rare whole family gatherings are still filled with humor, charades, old jokes, riddles, and stories.

There are a number of books in print about the value of humor. The Humor Project runs a conference every year to encourage everyone to add more laughter to their lives. If you are interested in ideas about how to add positive humor to your life, check their web site for more information www.humorproject.com.

3. Be able to read, write, and do basic math and be willing to upgrade skills as needed

You do not need a college or university degree to teach your child at home. You do need a basic proficiency in reading, writing, and math. If you can read children's picture books aloud, if you can write a letter, and if you can balance your checkbook, you have the basics I am talking about. Now don't panic about the checkbook balancing. Can you multiply, divide, and do addition and subtraction? Good enough.

As long as you can read, you can stay "one step ahead" of your children as you explore various areas of study by reading ahead on your own. You may feel that your understanding of some subjects is limited, and feel hesitant to attempt to teach these subjects. One thing to keep in mind is that one of the best ways to learn something is to teach it. My own understanding of things like the rotation of the planets around the sun increased immensely as I answered my children's questions.

You may find that what gave you trouble when you were 12 years old and in elementary school is not as difficult now. It can be quite a relief to look at a Grade 6 math book and find that the problems aren't as hard as they were when you were in Grade 6.

On the other hand if you look at the textbook and don't understand, then you may need to update your skills. There are often courses available for adults through community colleges and/or correspondence courses. One of the joys of taking courses as an adult is that the instructors on the whole are working hard to have you succeed. You are not a captive audience, you are a paying consumer of their services. This can be quite a refreshing feeling! You might also find that you can teach yourself what you need to know after asking someone you trust to explain how to start. There are many ways to acquire the knowledge necessary to teach your child.

I found that learning as an adult was not fraught with the tensions I had when learning in school as a child. Learning as an adult has been more relaxed because I made the decision to learn something. I was not forced. However, I have not taken any formal courses where grades were given. Most of the courses I've taken have been offered through volunteer training and have been informal classes set up so that everyone could learn and succeed.

Since the first edition of this book was published, programs and materials geared toward homeschooling families have blossomed. Some people find it very helpful to use material such as text books or programmed curricula materials. Others find distance teacher based programs make them feel more comfortable in helping their children learn at home. Support groups in your local area can help you find the program and/or material that might fit for you and your family. And others find that they prefer following their child's interest in helping their children learn basic skills.

Children Learn What They Live

If children live with criticism,
They learn to condemn.
If children live with hostility,
They learn to fight.
If children live with ridicule,
They learn to be shy.
If children live with shame,
They learn to feel guilty.
If children live with encouragement,
They learn confidence.
If children live with tolerance,
They learn to be patient.
If children live with praise,
They learn to appreciate.
If children live with acceptance,
They learn to love.
If children live with approval,
They learn to like themselves.
If children live with honesty,
They learn truthfulness.
If children live with security,
They learn to have faith
in themselves and others.
If children live with friendliness,
They learn the world is a nice place
in which to live.

4. Have a commitment to a philosophy that leads you to home-school

I have a strong commitment to homeschooling. My philosophy developed from my experience as an aide in a grade 1 classroom in an inner city school when I was 20 years old. My first day on the job was quite a shock. I arrived early and was shown to the classroom where I had a chance to look around before school started and the children arrived. When the bell rang, there was no teacher! I was in quite a panic. I was in charge of the 26 six and seven year olds sitting at their desks, looking at me.

I didn't know what their routine was. I found no daily plan on the teacher's desk to help me. I had never been in a grade 1 classroom in the U.S. before, as I had lived in the Netherlands at that age. I can't remember exactly how I managed. I probably asked the children for their help so that I could follow their normal routine. After recess, one and a half hours later, the substitute teacher arrived. She took over for the rest of the day.

The school that hired me had a large grant from the Ford Foundation making it possible to hire aides for each classroom. Money to purchase equipment, materials, and supplies were provided for as well. It looked like an ideal situation. Many people then, 1968, and now, thought that if schools only had adequate funding, all the problems that beset schooling would be solved.

From my first day on the job, I began to realize that while enough money could make school a more pleasant place to be, it could not solve all the problems that children have learning in school. During the next six months it became more and more clear to me that while school was a place where some children could learn, it was not necessarily the best place for all children to learn. For some children, it was a place where although they learned, they were not learning the three "Rs" - reading, writing and 'rithmetic. Instead, they learned about who they were in comparison to others.

They learned that their parents' expectations and their teachers' expectations were sometimes in conflict. I found that what they were learning in the unrecognized curriculum of school culture jeopardized their faith in themselves and their ability to learn.

In order to understand more about children and what happens to them in school, I began to read a number of books about children in elementary schools. I had taken courses in early childhood education and child development at university. Now I wanted to know more about elementary education. Authors like John Holt (*How Children Learn* and *How Children Fail*) and Sylvia Ashton Warner (*Teacher*) provided me with much food for thought. It was at this time, working in a school that seemed to have everything a school could want, that I decided that if and when I had children they would not go to school. I would teach them at home for I was disheartened by what I saw.

The six months I spent working in an inner city school took place during a very impressionable time in my life. I enjoyed being with the children. I was fascinated to observe them working to master the art of reading. At the same time there was a sense of adventure in the school. A sense that the educators were trying new things to make a difference so that the children could succeed. The teacher and aide in the other grade 1 classroom were trying a method from England called Primary Integrated Schooling where children could choose what they wanted to work on from all the many materials available. There were few teacher led directives, just a creative environment.

All of this energy, all of these resources were directed toward improving education in inner city schools. It was exciting to be a part of all this. At the same time, I was aware of the tensions between parents and teachers. Most of the teachers were white, most of the aides were African American and 95% of the parents were African American. The teaching staff had a number of ideas about "whole language" type learning. The parents wanted their children to learn how to read, write, and to do math so that their children could succeed in life, and were uncertain about these new methods. The teachers felt that they knew better than the parents about the ways that children learn. The parents were not at all sure if they could trust the teachers and their ideas about how learning took place.

The students in my class varied in their ability to learn the material presented to them. Although many of them struggled to learn to read the grade 1 reader, all but two of them could read the graffiti painted on the walls in the neighborhood. I found myself questioning how sensible it was to place so many small children in a classroom with only two adults. I watched the interaction of the children in the class, the sorting that had been done by the children as to who was or was not acceptable. I wondered if all of this was necessary. I wondered too, about some of the children who were designated as having learning problems or behavioral problems. Was some of their behavior and lack of success in learning because they were not "bright" or was a classroom situation too stressful for them?

All these thoughts and observations rattled around in my head as I worked with these children. Many years later, I still think of these children - Tony (not his real name), who had a difficult time with the language arts tasks assigned to him. He was not yet ready to learn to read, but he loved listening to stories and singing. Then there was Patricia (not her real name) who had a difficult time grasping any information. Yet one day when playing with parquetry blocks, she made a most amazing symmetrical design that surprised and pleased both the teacher and me. We tried to find other ways to engage her in more learning activities but we couldn't find anything else that she could use to demonstrate her innate intelligence.

I wonder how their lives have turned out. Did the years in

that school help them to be better able to cope in the world? I hope so. I hope that the care and the attention, the genuine desire to make school a better place to learn made a difference in their lives.

My next job was as a director of a daycare center. It became clear to me that here, as in schools, there was something askew with the way we value children in our society. The daycare was subsidized and provided employment for six staff. Most of the parents of the children who came to the center worked in the shoe factories in the area earning the minimum wage. They dropped their children off at 6:30 a.m. and picked them up 8 to 10 hours later. The 20 children in the center spent more time with the staff than with their parents. I worked there for about four months, a temporary director until they could find a permanent director. I was offered the job permanently, but I was unable to commit myself to something that felt so wrong. I could not accept that I had so much influence in these children's lives. I knew that if I accepted the job on a permanent basis my heart would break. I wanted to change the way child care was funded so that subsidies for child care went directly to the mothers. I wanted to find ways to help women learn the nurturing skills they needed to be able to be home with their children and enjoy them.

I know that those four months were good months for the children. They were also good months for me. I began cooking their lunches instead of buying them from a school lunch program. Whole foods gradually became a staple, no more Wonder bread! I baked bread for the center, the children helped and we had a good time doing this together. The janitor enjoyed the bread so much that he began to join us in the baking. Soon, he took over and started baking all the bread for us - half white/half whole wheat flour.

It was summer time, and we went swimming everyday. The

children then returned to the center and had naps if they were under six or rested if they were over six. Most of them fell asleep
because they had gotten up so early. When their parents came to
pick them up, it was usually quiet. I made a point of being available
with a plate of cookies and lemonade to let them know what their
child had done that day. I asked the parents if they objected to the
naps, if it made harder for the children to go to sleep in the evening.
All of them said that although the children went to bed a little later,
they were pleased to pick up children who were not tired and cranky.
They appreciated the chance to talk with me and slow down a few
minutes before going home to start supper. My heart went out to
each of them.

It seemed to me that these parents were caught in a bind (as
are many parents today) that has no easy solution. Both daycare
and school are places where, for good or ill, children are raised by
people other than their parents. Children learn attitudes, values,
and ways of relating from their caretakers. This curriculum is un-
spoken and not acknowledged and has tremendous influence in
children's lives.

I know that for many people, there are no alternatives to
school and daycare. I know that for too many children, school and
daycare is a safer place than home. And this both saddens me and
makes me angry. I know that as a society we have the resources to
make children's lives safe. We have the resources to support and
encourage parents to learn to nurture their children. We just don't
seem to be able to make the commitment to do so.

Many years passed before I had children. During those
years, I was a nursery school teacher, swimming instructor and self-
sufficient farmer. I enjoyed being with children. I had friends who
homeschooled their children. I had many opportunities to talk with
them about why they made the choice to keep their children at
home instead of sending them to school. All of these experiences

strengthened my earlier decision that if I ever had children I would not send them to school. Fortunately Larry, my husband and the father of my children, felt the same way.

Even though I felt so strongly about homeschooling, there were days when I had young children that I wanted nothing more than the peace and quiet that children attending school for part of the day would give me. I struggled to meet the various needs of my children and wondered if it was all worth while. As I struggled, I would remember why I made this decision and remember that the reasons I decided to homeschool still applied even though it involved hard work for me.

Robin, Marty, Holly, Noah, Josh

I believe that children learn best in an atmosphere where they are respected, loved and valued. I think it is important to encourage children to listen to their own inner voice. I think it is important that children have the opportunity to move at their own pace to master the skills needed to be competent in the world. I know that all children are inherently good and want to move toward mastering the skills they need in order to function. I believe that children need a structure in which to live, but a structure that is responsive to a child's cycles and takes them into account. I believe that children need adults around them who model integrity. I believe that children need adults who relate to them in respectful, caring ways so that a child can learn to relate in respectful and caring ways. I think that it is vital for a child to feel "safe" in his or her learning environment. At the same time, other people in the family also need to feel "safe." I feel strongly that given the opportunity and support needed, children will find their gifts.

Everyone who homeschools chooses this method of education for various reasons and philosophies. I've outlined the basics of my philosophy not to convince you but to let you know how and why I made the decisions I did about education. What is important is to have a strong commitment, a philosophy, as to why you are homeschooling your children. There are going to be many times when being a homeschooling mother will be a challenge. Your commitment will help you to ground your frustrations and put them into the perspective of your long range goals. (You may wish to use the information in the appendix on goal setting to help you define what your goals are in parenting and homeschooling your children.)

Having a philosophy behind your decision to homeschool also gives you direction. If you homeschool only because you think the school system is terrible, then you are reacting to the school system. This can give you the courage and strength to make a change in the beginning, but over time, a choice that is a reaction tends to cause more reactions. I, personally, like to act rather than to re-act. Re-acting can help us try something new, but it is just the opposite side of the coin from what we are re-acting to. It is not a change, it is a flip, a swing of the pendulum from one side to the other.

Finding your own positive reasons to homeschool can help you to formulate your own homeschooling philosophy. Your philosophy can then form a basis for your actions. Actions are a way of going beyond the swinging pendulum to a new place. When we act, we can have more freedom to choose the things we want to do based on their suitability rather than choosing to do something in reaction to its opposite. It is a way of going between the two sides of the coin rather than going from one side to the other.

A homeschooling philosophy helps you to put your educational decisions in context.

5. Be willing to develop communication/listening skills

Communication is the key to any relationship. When your child was a baby, although he or she could not use words to express him/herself, you learned how to interpret and listen to his or her cues. As your child grows older and more competent in making him/herself understood and begins to ask more complex questions, you will also need to develop your ability to communicate more clearly. I thought that I was fairly adept at communicating. I found to my dismay that I often confused my children with information that I thought was clear but they found confusing. I also found that my listening skills were not as good as I would have liked. I realized how often I talked rather than listened.

I think that listening is the key to effective parenting and homeschooling. Listening doesn't mean limiting yourself to the words a child is saying. It also means listening to the body language and underlying feelings. This kind of listening is like the picking up of cues that one does with a small baby. Perhaps you can remember when your child was a baby. Before he or she would cry there was a series of cues he or she gave that let you know that crying was imminent. Cues continue beyond the baby years. The more in tune you are with your child's cues, the easier it is to understand and communicate with your child.

One of the most effective ways I've found to really listen to a child is to try to see things from a child's point of view, to remove my agenda from the situation. This often brings me a fresh perspective.

6. Be prepared to receive criticism for your decision to homeschool

For many homeschoolers, the decision to homeschool is one that causes great upheavals and concern among extended family members. Grandparents, aunts, uncles, brothers, sisters, etc. all feel like they must say something and express their concern that you have made this choice. Homeschooling your child is a parenting decision that can affect the extended members of your family because it is so visible.

For example, grandparents may find that their friends ask "How is your grandchild doing in school?" If they are uncomfortable answering this question, they will more than likely pass on their discomfort to you as a criticism of your choice to homeschool.

It might be helpful to prepare your extended family by letting them know why you have made the decision to homeschool. When you give them this information, let them know you are not expecting to persuade them one way or the other, you are just informing them. Giving extended family members information about why you are homeschooling and not expecting agreement may ease tensions. Impart this information to family members when no children are present. Make it clear to extended family members that if they have concerns about homeschooling, the concerns need to be expressed to you not to your child or children.

All of this sounds very calm, logical and reasonable, and I wish I could have been calm, logical and reasonable each time someone questioned my choices. Fortunately, I had already made so many different choices before having children that my choice to homeschool did not surprise my extended family. I received very little criticism for our choice to homeschool from extended family members. The criticism I received in the early years came from friends and acquaintances. This was at times quite devastating, yet when I weighed the criticism against my inner convictions, I saw that it was my desire to be liked by everyone that was threatened by people's criticism. Being liked by everyone has never been my goal.

When someone questioned my decision regarding homeschooling, I found that it was more helpful if I discussed the positive aspects of homeschooling rather than the negatives of school. The positive reasons are often easier for someone to accept. Some people were threatened by my choice to homeschool and felt that it was a criticism of their choice of education for their children. When I stated the reasons for my choices in positive terms based on my feelings and perceptions, then, although the people I spoke with might disagree, it was often easier for them to accept my choice.

I remember an exchange I had with a teacher who could not understand why I wouldn't want to put my children in her class. I asked her if she enjoyed her job. She said she did. I asked her if she enjoyed helping children learn to read. She did. I told her that I enjoyed that, too. I liked being a part of the process of my child learning to read or learning other things about the world. I enjoyed being able to observe the insights that my children had as they connected one thing with another. She seemed more relaxed after that conversation. My reasons for homeschooling were not against her or other members of the teaching profession. My reasons were personal and positive, similar to her reasons for choosing to be a teacher.

If withstanding criticism for your choice to homeschool is a bit scary for you, you might want to consider taking a course in self-esteem, assertiveness, and/or communication skills. Part of maturing is accepting that some of the choices you make about how you live your life may offend others. This happens to every-one. Homeschooling can be a way to find strengths you weren't aware of as you find ways to stay true to your own beliefs while at the same time accepting that others may not agree with you. As my children grew older, I didn't feel as vulnerable. I had *proof of the pudding,* my children are capable, self-motivated learners, able to listen and converse with others, "coachable," and delightful people to be around.

7. Have a support system or network and/or a supportive partner

One of the main criticisms I heard when Josh was about 6 years old was that I was being too overprotective and had my children tied to my apron strings. This kind of comment would disturb my equilibrium for quite awhile. I felt so defensive, so vul-nerable. I found it essential to have other women to talk to who, while they might not have made the decision to homeschool, did choose to have close relationships with their children. I joined a group that supported me in my choice of mothering my children. This contact with other women who were also exploring what it meant to have close, loving relationships with their children helped me to feel less isolated.

La Leche League was my support group for many years. Although as an organization it is dedicated to helping mothers breastfeed their babies, it is also a group that supports mothers in meeting the needs of their babies and children - a unique thing in our North American culture that focuses more on adult needs than on children's needs.

I learned from a friend in La Leche League to laugh when someone suggested that I had my children tied to my apron strings. Her response was always "You're darn right. And I've got them tied good and tight, too." I found that agreeing with someone often took the wind out of his or her sails, broke the tension, and allowed the conversation to move on.

Your support system can be for homeschooling and/or for mothering. It doesn't need to be big - a few close friends can make a big difference if they are able to listen and support you in your choices. In many places there are meetings for homeschoolers where homeschooling issues are discussed. Some people find these helpful. If you try one homeschooling support group and it doesn't quite suit you, try another one. On-line support groups for homeschooling abound. Many people find these virtual communities helpful and a great resource.

Do some exploring and see what you can find in your community. If you live in a rural area and can't find anyone close by, check your library for information about homeschooling networks. Reaching out to others helps you to feel less isolated. Talking with other women about homeschooling or other mothering concerns can give you a different perspective on your situation. You may find that friends who have not made the same educational choice can still offer a listening ear and support.

La Leche League succeeds because it is a place where women share their stories. Mothers of very young babies hear the stories of mothers whose babies are slightly older. Sharing the struggles, problems, challenges, and joys of mothering allows all the mothers at these meetings to put their personal experience in a context and see their lives as part of a bigger picture. Sharing your concerns and worries about homeschooling with someone who has lived through some similar worries can help you feel more comfortable and may help you find solutions that hadn't occurred to you. Each child is different. Each family is different, yet we all have common themes of concern. Having a place to air those concerns can help you find your own unique way to address that concern and find what works best for you. That's one of the best things about homeschooling - each family finds unique ways to homeschool. There are probably as many ways to homeschool as there are people who do it.

One of the benefits for you when you homeschool your children is that you have time to form a network of supportive friends. You have time to form deep and valuable friendships with other like-minded women that you might not have had time for if you were doing some other kind of work. Your children can play together and you can share ideas, worries, things that worked, things that didn't work, help each other figure out why something didn't work as well as explore new ideas.

Be sure that the support group you have is actually supportive. In other words, air your grievances about homeschooling only to those who have no vested interest in you changing your method of education. If your mother is quite concerned about you not sending your daughter to school, she would not be a good person to talk to when you feel that you are at the end of your rope with your daughter. Even if the thing that is driving you crazy might be typical behavior for an 8 year old girl, your mother may tell you that "If only you sent her to school, this would not be a problem."

When we choose to raise our children in ways that are different from the culture around us, then whatever behavior a child shows that might be irritating to his elders is usually attributed to whatever we are doing that is different from the dominant culture. It happens that way for women who nurse their babies. "The baby is doing this because you nurse him all the time" is a comment many mothers have heard from a critical relative when whatever the baby is doing is normal baby behavior but not a behavior that this person approves of or likes. It is so easy for someone who disapproves of your decision to homeschool to attribute any behavior of your child that you find hard to cope with a result of homeschooling. When you are struggling to understand a child's behavior, this way of attributing the behavior to your choice to homeschool is not supportive.

Many times, as I struggled to understand my child's behavior, I wondered whether the behavior was due to:

homeschooling

typical for the age or

influenced by factors I did not even know about.

If you find that those you turn to for support are suggesting that your problems could be easily solved by changing your method of education, you might want to find another support person who can allow you to think things through without having a ready-made solution for your problems.

Learning about child development can also provide support for your own perceptions and observations of your children. Keep in mind that some of what is considered normal child development for children of school age and beyond may be school induced development and not necessarily a natural part of child development.

School culture is so dominant that those who do research in the field of child development are often not aware of the influence of school culture. They describe some of children's developmental behavior as human development when in actuality it is developmental behavior taking place in the context of going to school. Those who study child development are becoming aware of the importance of taking into consideration cultural bias when studying children in different parts of the world. It will take time for people to realize that school is a culture as well and that it influences a child's development.

A book that I found interesting and informative regarding children's development is *Your Child's Growing Mind: A Guide to Learning and Brain Development from Birth to Adolescence* by Jane M. Healy,

Ph.D. This book is a compilation of a number of current theories of nervous system development and how this information applies to how children learn. I found it confirmed my own observation of my children. The author has also written a book that addresses schooling and the need for change within schools that seems to me to speak eloquently on behalf of homeschooling. (The author tried to teach her child at home and found it did not work for her. She draws the conclusion from her one experience that teaching a child at home will not work for anyone else either. Her conclusion about homeschooling clearly illustrates how important it is to avoid making blanket statements.)

I found the information about cognitive development in her book fascinating. The information in the book can be used as a gauge to determine how realistic your expectations for certain learning tasks are for a child of a particular age.

Learning more about child development can help you deal with criticism as well as help you to be a better homeschooling mother. If you can state that "Studies show that children of this age vary in their ability to do math," your critic hears that you are knowledgeable. People usually express criticism out of their concern. Grandmas and grandpas want their grandchildren to have the best chance to do well in life. Homeschooling may be difficult for them to accept because it is so different from what they did as parents.

Using empathetic listening skills when someone is criticizing your choice of education is an option that may also be helpful. Empathetic listening is a way of listening for the feeling in the words that someone is expressing, i.e., "What do you mean you're not sending her to school? How will she ever be able to cope in the world and get a job?" Empathetic response "When you think about her future you're worried that she won't be able to make it." As an empathetic listener, you don't take what the speaker is saying personally, as something you need to defend, fix, or explain. Instead, you respond with empathy and concern for the speaker's feelings.

There are a number of books that have been written about this kind of listening: *People Skills* by Robert Bolton and *How To Talk So Kids Will Listen and Listen So Kids Will Talk* by Adele Faber and Elaine Mazlish are two that I have found particularly helpful. It's amazing how often an empathetic response allows the focus of a conversation to change.

When your empathy is genuine, it means that you are listening and walking in that other person's shoes. You are not trying to either defend your point of view or change the other person's point of view. It's a very useful communication tool. Learning empathetic listening skills is like learning a new language. It takes practice to acquire the skills needed to do it well. It is worth taking time to become proficient in this new language. It will help your communication with your children as well as with those who may criticize you.

Empathy means to listen without an agenda - listening with your heart open to the emotions behind the words.

If you have a partner/husband, homeschooling will be less draining for you if you and your partner agree to homeschool. Two people may agree to homeschool and yet have two entirely different ideas of what this means. It is important for you and your partner to talk about expectations for the children and the issues involved such as:

who is responsible for what
is this an experiment and does it have a time limit
what are the criteria we will use to judge if this is
      working
will we do school at home, child-led learning, etc.

Discussing these issues enable you to see where you agree and where you may disagree about homeschooling. It will take time to resolve any differences. How well you can work together even when you disagree depends on your commitment both to the idea of homeschooling and your relationship. Each couple works this out over time. The goal would be to find a way that you can support each other as you homeschool your children.

Homeschooling can be a strain on a marriage. It more than likely means one income, or the equivalent of one income as someone needs to be with the child (children) all the time. It means that there will be child oriented activities all through the day and into the evening, as well as children's toys and materials being a more prevalent part of the household. It may mean that mom needs time to herself and only gets it at night when the children are in bed asleep. There may be less couple time. I am not trying to discourage anyone from homeschooling. I am trying to give you a realistic picture of the stresses and strains of having children around 24 hours a day.

I know women who have homeschooled although their partners have not been 100% supportive. Their commitment to provide a learning environment suited to their children's needs was so strong that they were willing to risk their relationship with their partner.

My husband started teaching in 1968. His years of teaching experience with grades 3-12 and many children of various abilities was a great asset for me. He was a great resource for both materials and maintaining perspective. I can't imagine how it would have been to homeschool without his support, encouragement, and involvement.

This does not mean that we did not have struggles. We did, many of them! However, these struggles have more to do with the struggles that most couples face when they have children and live together - issues about emotions, housework, sex, time, and space. On the issue of homeschooling, we've been in accord. Because we saw eye to eye on the issues of homeschooling, we have learned to work together on other issues.

Stages of learning

We all come to a new venture with a great deal of hope and many expectations about how it's going to work. I found it helpful to know that people seem to acquire the ability to do thing in stages. Let me use the example that Kathleen Auerbach, RN and Lactation Consultant, used when she presented this idea at a La Leche League Conference. She was speaking about how mothers acquire the ability to mother. She used an example from her own early months as a mother, which as you can tell from the story, happened more than 25 years ago.

In the first stage of learning, we think there is only one way to do something. A diaper salesman came to Kathleen's house when she was pregnant with her first child and showed her how to fold a diaper. She had not folded diapers before, so she assumed that "This is the way to fold diapers." After her baby was born, she always folded his diapers precisely the way she had been shown by that diaper salesman.

In the second stage of learning, we begin to experiment. Kathleen found that every once in a while she didn't manage to fold the diaper exactly as shown and nothing terrible happened. The diaper still fulfilled its function.

The third stage of learning is the mastery stage where we

see that we can make of this situation what we like based on our own observations and experience. Kathleen realized that as long as the diaper was attached to her baby, it would serve its function. How it was folded was not as vital as she once thought. Reviewing that process of acquiring a new skill:

Stage 1 - Beginning Stage
There's only one way to do something.
Stage 2 - Experimentation Stage
Let's see if this will work if I try this another way.
Stage 3 - Mastery Stage
I have incorporated my own experience to do this my way.

Each of us goes through similar stages as we acquire new information and learn. One of the most challenging things about working with children is that just when we feel that we have mastered how to mother a 2 month old, a child grows and changes. We must start again and go through these stages to learn how to mother a 6 month old, etc.

When we start to homeschool, we have a picture of how it is going to be and how it will work. I remember when Josh was 3½ years old. I was having a very difficult time. I wasn't getting the response from him that I expected. I had been a nursery school teacher. I thought I should be an expert with this age. I remembered mothers of the students in my nursery school marveling at how patient I was with their children and how responsive their children were to me. I found, much to my chagrin, that now that I was the mother of a 3½ year old, I had very little patience. I felt concern for Josh because I ran out of patience so often.

I spoke with my husband at length one evening and shared my worries and concerns. I suggested that contrary to my strong stand on homeschooling perhaps we should send Josh to nursery school. There he would have people around him who weren't always being frustrated with him. During our discussion, something shifted for me. I realized that I was holding so tightly to the idea of what a 3½ year old should be like and what a mother of a 3½ year old should be like, that I couldn't see Josh for who he was. I managed to let go of the strangle hold my ideas had on my ability to respond to my child. My perception shifted. Whatever had been driving me over the edge no longer had that power.

I was grateful that my husband could listen to me in such a supportive way even though he felt very strongly about the importance of homeschooling. He helped me to find a solution to my dilemma that didn't involve another dilemma, conflicting belief systems. He helped me to work through the various stages of learning by just listening to me and allowing me to express my emotions about the situation. This enabled me to see that my picture of being the mother of a 3½ year old and having a 3½ year old was like having to fold the diaper a certain way - it wasn't quite that rigid. I could find my own way by responding to my child instead of trying to fit him into my preconceived ideas.

8. Be able to learn from mistakes

My children know that making mistakes is a natural part of learning. They are not afraid to make mistakes when they try something new. They know that there are many ways to go about solving a problem and that not every problem has one "right" answer.

A baby learning to walk makes many "mistakes" and falls down. Eventually, through trial and error, persistence, and practice, the baby learns to walk. Each "mistake" helped the child to learn that "no, this doesn't work, I have to try a slightly different way of balancing to stay moving and upright." The difficult thing for me to accept is that while I was learning how to be a mother, I

made mistakes on my children. I can get quite carried away by the
mistakes I made and focus exclusively on those things I wish I had
not done. I can't seem to let go of them. I read something in
Mastering Your Hidden Self by Serge King that has helped me to learn
to accept my mistakes and learn from them.

"Repentance, which may include atonement, has been greatly
misunderstood. It is almost always interpreted as meaning 'to feel
sorry or miserable about what you have done.' That doesn't do
you or anyone else any good. What repentance really means is to
change your way of thinking and to act differently. Just to feel
sorry is meaningless; you have to do something about it. That
something may be an attitude you can change or an act you can
perform quite on your own, or it may have to involve someone
else, in which case it is called 'atonement.'

"Now atonement is another word that has been greatly misunderstood. It is usually taken to mean that you have to 'pay back'
a person or society or even God for something you did wrong,
and this paying back can be in the form of money, a good deed, or
the undergoing of punishment. All of this is a distortion. Atonement actually means 'to become reconciled' (i.e., 'friendly again,'
from the Middle English 'at one', 'in accord') or 'to make amends.'
The latter term, 'amends,' means 'to improve one's conduct,' not
to make up for something or to pay something (c.f. Webster's).

"The third step in forgiveness, absolution (the same thing as
pardon) comes from a Latin word meaning 'to set free,' and is
essentially a declaration that one is set free from guilt, blame or
obligation.

"In practical terms to forgive yourself, you acknowledge your
mistakes, change your ways, and make the decision to pardon yourself. Of course it is nice if someone else pardons you, but that
won't have any effect unless you accept it, so it all comes down to
pardoning yourself. If feeling guilty is habitual, even if you have
changed your ways, then you will have to replace it with the habit
of feeling pardoned. If you have the belief that you should be
punished, then you must either eliminate the 'should' idea from
your consciousness or find a way to punish yourself once that will

be effective in convincing your ku (subconscious) that it's enough while not being too harmful." (from page 93. See page 34 of *Mastering Your Hidden Self* for a more complete definition of Ku. Used by permission of the author, Serge King)

I find this approach helps me when I get depressed about some of the things I did when my children were younger. It helps me to know that changing my behavior is repentance. It helps me to remember that in order for me to model that it is OK to make mistakes, I need to be gentle with myself when I make them.

Being able to accept my own mistakes leads me to look at the judgments I have made about myself. Do I, deep down inside myself, really believe that I am a *good* person or do I believe that I am *bad*? Depending on my answer, I can give myself permission to not know something or to not understand something, or I can look at my mistake as proof that I am *bad*.

You may wonder what this has to do with homeschooling. Why is it important to look at the way you treat yourself when you make a mistake? If you are homeschooling your children, your attitude toward mistakes becomes the atmosphere in which your children learn. That is why I think it is important to look at this issue. Alice Miller, in her later books *Banished Knowledge* and *Breaking the Wall of Silence* discusses how difficult it is for us as adults to deal in a positive way with mistakes because accepting mistakes, acknowledging them, means facing our own unresolved pain as children when people/parents blamed us for the mistakes we made.

When my two older boys were little, I would sometimes think that their actions, which were typical for their age, were motivated by intentions of wanting to hurt or cause pain. In other words, I sometimes assumed that their intentions were *bad*. When I would take the time to think about this and look underneath my assumptions of their behavior, I knew that my children weren't *bad*. How could they be, they did not have the depth of experience needed to act with any *bad* intent.

But in the heat of two little boys fighting with each other, I would loose my rational perspective. It has taken me years of thinking this through, and observing my children to see how often I infer a motive for an action that says more about me than about my child. This thinking and observing is part of the work Alice Miller talks about in her books.

A six year old who is being bothered might throw something at the person who's bothering him. Throwing things at people (except as part of playing some sort of game like baseball, basketball, etc.) is not acceptable behavior in our house. When this happened, I would intervene and help my child learn a more acceptable way to express his anger and frustration at being bothered. However, the behavior does not mean that the child is *bad*.

I read about this idea (a child's behavior is not necessarily a reflection of his/her character) many times in many books about parenting. I read again and again that a child needs to be shown how to express anger, rage, and frustration appropriately. It took me many hours of thought to discover how to really apply this truth when mothering my children. What helped me to work through this was constantly referring to my belief that all children are inherently *good*. I had to go through the three stages of learning that I described earlier many times before I finally got it.

Assigning inappropriate motives to children's behavior is part and parcel of the pedagogy of child-rearing in our Western patriarchal belief system. Let me illustrate with an example from when Josh was a toddler under two years old. At that time, Josh had a desperate desire to communicate with words and had a difficult time pronouncing the words he wanted to use. Someone who observed Josh at this time commented to me that this difficulty was a sign of his laziness and my over-responsiveness to him. Josh didn't talk because he didn't need to talk. I responded to him even though he wasn't talking clearly. I was rendered speechless by this comment! It was so obvious to me that the person who said this had not observed Josh very closely. He would sometimes be in tears because I couldn't quite interpret what he wanted to say. He tried so hard to communicate and be understood!

The philosophy that this view represents - that children are lazy and must be made to learn - is very strong in our North American society. Even though I consciously do not believe this is true, I sometimes catch myself operating as though it were true. When this happens, I remind myself that a child wants to gain competency and wants to be able to function in the world. Blaming a child for making mistakes and labeling him as lazy is not conducive to learning.

Many children do not follow the time table for learning or competency that adults have in mind. When this happens, adults will frequently begin to make assumptions about why a child is not learning certain things, as in the example above. This can lead to all sorts of incriminations and assumptions about a child's motives that can lead a child to refuse to learn anything at all in order to maintain his sense of control over himself.

As my children have made mistakes in the process of learning to read and do math, I would remind myself of the necessity of making mistakes. A child is not deliberately driving an adult crazy when she doesn't understand something. A different approach needs to be found so that the child can grasp the ideas presented.

Let me illustrate this point with an incident that my brother remembers from his first weeks in kindergarten. Our family moved from the Netherlands to the U.S. in 1956. My brother was 5 years old at the time. About three weeks after our arrival, he started kindergarten. He didn't speak English, so he didn't understand the kindergarten teacher when she spoke to him. He remembers that she would start to yell at him because he could not understand. She would get louder and louder and more and more angry, implying that he was "dumb" because he didn't understand her. He remembers wondering what was wrong with her. Why couldn't she speak to him in Dutch? He could communicate just fine with his sisters and parents.

We often get louder and angrier when a child does not understand. Perhaps just as my brother did not understand the language the teacher was speaking, our children don't understand our language and we need to find a way to communicate in their language. We need to trust in their ability to achieve mastery and allow them to make mistakes and learn from those mistakes just as they did when they were learning to walk. We also need to trust in our own development and learn from the mistakes we make.

9. Be willing to develop limit-setting skills

As a mother, it is essential to acquire the ability to set limits and/or define boundaries. As a homeschooling mother, this skill is even more vital. I once heard someone say to me about a homeschooled child "No wonder that child doesn't go to school. He is totally unruly and disruptive. Nobody would let him stay in school." This surprised me as I had not equated unruly children and homeschooling. After hearing this comment I began to think of how homeschooling could lead to unruly children. I realized that in making the decision to homeschool, many parents are searching for a more free-flowing form of education with no adult imposed learning agenda. Because there is a swing away from an adult imposed learning agenda, any form of adult expectations is also discarded and there are no guidelines for behavior. This leads to chaos and an overwhelmed family.

While I believe strongly that children need to have room to learn at their own rate, children also need to live within expectations of responsible and caring behavior. In other words, while I do not expect my children to master reading by a certain age, I do expect them to behave in such a way that makes it safe for everyone in our household - no hitting, biting, throwing, etc. While this standard of behavior is expected, I am also aware that a child may be able to understand something (like no hitting) long before she or he may be able to act on it. In the face of angry feelings, my children needed help to be able follow our family rules.

To set limits and family rules, you need to respect your children and yourself - to feel as though you are worthy of being treated with kindness and consideration. In other words, you can treat your children with respect and still have children who are unaware of other's needs and requirements, if you do not also teach your child to treat you and others with respect. This word "respect" can have such negative connotations that I want to demonstrate what I mean with an example.

When a small child climbs on mom's lap and sits there, he sometimes hurts his mom by kicking and/or pinching as he climbs up or hurts her by bumping up and down on her lap once he gets there. This behavior is not intended to hurt. The small child is unaware of the effect his actions have. To begin to teach a child to show respect for you, his mother, it is important for you to let the child know that this hurts. You might say something like, "When you climb up on me this way, it hurts me. If you want to get up on my lap, just tell me and I will pick you up." You show your child affection at the same time that you are setting a limit - Mommy is not for hurting.

The next time your small child begins to climb up on your lap and it hurts, you stop him, remove him from the climbing position he's in, lift him up on your leg, and say again, "It hurts me when you climb up on me like that. Mommies are not for hurting." You may need to have this conversation a hundred times, a thousand times. Each time you have this interchange you stick to your limit and respond to your child's need to sit in your lap. If you can anticipate when the climbing is going to happen, then that's all the better. You have sidestepped one of the steps and progressed to a new step by lifting your child as soon as he looks like he would like to be on your lap.

If a child persists in hurting, it is time to look at how you give attention to your child. Does your child only receive attention when he hurts you? Give him your positive attention by playing with him. Go outside and run about or read a story together, lifting your child up into your lap or something else that gives your child your focused attention. This stops the need to get attention by hurting you. The reason hurting works is because we respond. A child learns quickly just what will make his mother respond to him.

The book *Don't Shoot The Dog* by Karen Prior has very helpful information about positive reinforcement and how to use it effectively. The author is an animal trainer and draws on her experience to explain how to use positive reinforcement effectively. She mentions in this book that among animal trainers there is a suggestion that people not be allowed to have children until they can teach a chicken to dance. That always gave me food for thought.

I used a young child for my example of how to set a limit because it is when children are young that we begin to demonstrate how to treat others with respect and courtesy. As you meet your child's need for attention and your physical presence, you make it clear when something hurts or is uncomfortable for you with actions as well as words. If you do not let your child know when something he is doing hurts, you are doing your child a disservice.

Small children need physical contact with their parents. They are not aware that their actions can be hurtful. They need guidance to show them how they can have this close physical contact so that it is pleasant for both the child and the parent. You define what is acceptable behavior for your child (Mommies are not for hurting) and you help your child learn this behavior by lovingly reminding him when necessary with both your actions and your words.

For small children in particular it is your actions - picking up your child as he starts to climb up on your lap or helping him climb up so that it doesn't hurt - that is important. Words are not enough. You need to show your child what you mean. This establishes clear and effective communication. You are not asking your children to read your mind or interpret your body language. You set limits that define for your child how to climb or sit on your lap.

Young children who have had limits established for them in an atmosphere of love and respect grow into older children who are comfortable with reasonable limits. Let me give you an example: Robin (who was 12 years old at the time) and his friend, Robert, (almost 12 years old) were riding their bikes through an obstacle course they had set up in our back yard. I was getting ready to take my older boys to the golf course. I had a number of things I needed to do before I could go. I asked Josh to tell them that I needed them to stop riding their bikes while I was gone and come in the house and have some lunch. The two boys readily agreed to this. They could see the sense of not engaging in such a challenging big muscle activity when they were home by themselves. I was gone about 30 minutes. As soon as I came back the boys went out again and started riding.

Limit setting involves thinking ahead to how a child might respond in a certain situation and being prepared. The old adage "An ounce of prevention is worth a pound of cure" could have been thought of just for mothers. Limit setting means defining what is not acceptable behavior, saying "no," it also means defining what is acceptable behavior, saying "yes."

Let me give you an another example. I took my daughter, Holly, with me to a couple of weekend long meetings when she was 5 and 6 years old. Before going, we talked about what she could expect - that I would be talking and listening in meetings. We needed to think about the things she could bring so that she could play quietly. She could climb into my lap and do things sitting in my lap, but I would not be able to read to her during the meetings. I explained that during my breaks I would read or do things just with her and that we would go to the zoo together before the meetings started.

Holly thought she could do this. She looked forward to the trip to the zoo because she was interested in animals. I knew she could manage during the meetings because she had entertained herself at other shorter meetings.

We flew on an airplane, arrived early, went to the zoo and were ready for the meetings when they started. She was the only child present and managed quite well. She had my physical presence even though she did not have my undivided attention. She climbed into my lap to draw pictures or play with playdough when she needed to. We talked briefly at various times when she needed help with things. During my breaks, she had my attention. We went swimming, read a story, or did something that she wanted to do. We had a good time together. She understood what was expected of her before we left because we talked about it at length before hand. I showed her the limits of the situation and prepared us both by talking about what she could expect. We planned together what toys she brought along. The other adults were delighted by her presence.

My daughter was not ready to be separated from me for a whole weekend at that time. I wasn't ready for that either, knowing how much she still needed my sheer physical presence. I knew that she would be able to entertain herself as long as we brought the right toys; I made sure to spend some focused time with her throughout each day; and we spent time together at night.

Although she didn't have my attention as much as she would

have liked, she did have my presence. She was also old enough to see that although it was tiresome to be in the meetings, we did some special things both before and after the meetings like going to the zoo or swimming in the hotel pool. She was able to accept the limits of the situation. Had she not been able to do this, I would have chosen not to go because neither one of us was ready for that long a period of separation.

A year later, when Noah (who was almost 14 years old at the time) was diagnosed with Type I diabetes, I stayed with him in the hospital for 11 days. My husband stayed home from work and brought Holly to the hospital everyday. She was 7 years old and understood how much Noah needed me. She expressed her anguish about not being with me in tears, especially when leaving to go home. She also told me that when she was home it wasn't as bad as when she was saying good-bye to me at the hospital. She was able to express and deal with the mixture of feelings she had. I was able to listen to her feelings and not discredit them.

As my children learned to live within the limits I set on their behavior, they also learned that I listened to them, to their need to be heard and considered. That is what respect is all about. *Webster's II New Riverside Dictionary* definition of respect "To feel or show deferential regard for: esteem." I cannot teach my child about self-respect or self-esteem without also teaching him to hold others in esteem - to be respectful of others.

While I expected my children to treat others with the same consideration and courtesy with which they would like to be treated, I also accepted that they are children and will make mistakes. I was learning (motherhood provides many opportunities to learn) and I was a lot older than they were. It takes practice to do anything well. Living in a family and homeschooling offers a great opportunity to practice showing care and consideration for oneself and others.

Many questions of "who gets to do what when" come up

when you have more than one person living in a household. Sorting out family values and philosophy is something that all parents do. As a homeschooling mother, you spend more time with your children, so more situations will come up that require you to define the family's values and philosophy. It can be quite challenging! At the same time, one of the greatest benefits of homeschooling is that you can form your family's values and philosophy without the constant bombardment of contrasting values that school often presents to many children. One of the concerns I have heard parents express when their child starts school at age 5 is the difficulty their child has sorting out the different expectations and values school presents.

For example, when a child at home wants to ask a question, he finds a parent and asks. At school, he must raise his hand and be recognized by his teacher before asking his question. The teacher will only recognize the child at certain times. Sometimes, children are discouraged from asking questions because it disrupts the flow of what the teacher is doing, or age peers may tease a child about his questions. A child who has been encouraged to be curious and has had his questions seriously considered and answered might find the teacher's and his age peers' response to his questions confusing. Over time, a child adjusts and learns when to ask questions and, depending on how vulnerable he is to his age peers, whether he asks questions at all. Homeschooling offers the opportunity to limit the conflicting values a young child faces.

This does not mean that there won't ever be any conflicting values for a homeschooled child. I can remember a baseball coach suggesting to me that my sons needed to be more aggressive when playing ball. If there was someone in the way on the base path, they should just learn to run him down. My boys were not interested in running someone down to improve their baseball skills. The coach thought that it made good baseball sense to do this. My sons disagreed. They didn't think that risking injury made good baseball sense, nor did it suit their personal style.

In setting limits for children, you also model how they can set limits for themselves - an important skill to have. It is OK to say "no" to your child. You will also have your child saying "no" to you. Although we may at times want instant compliance from a child, we need to be aware of how important it is for a child to be able to say "no" to an adult. If we want our children to be able to listen to their own inner voice, we have to expect that there will be conflict between what we want a child to do and what that child wants to do. Listening and negotiating are all part of the skills you practice as a mother. As a homeschooling mother, you'll have even more opportunities to practice this skill. At the same time, because you will be spending more time with your children and have less random outside influence, you may find that after the initial hard work of defining family rules, you will have more time to enjoy the benefits of your children's respect and consideration for themselves, each other, and you as they grow older.

10. Be willing to develop patience

Many people say to me, "Oh, I could never teach my children. I don't have the patience." They comment on my patience and assume that this is a quality that I was born with. Certainly, if you don't have any interest in learning patience, homeschooling your children would not be a good idea. However, if you are will-ing to **develop** patience, homeschooling provides many opportu-nities to do so.

I found breathing to be one of the best things to do when I had exhausted my patience. Over time, I have developed ways to be patient. Patience doesn't mean being a martyr. It means being willing to give things time, including yourself. When I run out of patience, I try to change what I am doing rather than losing my temper. I try to be aware of when my patience is real and when it is not.

When my two older boys were younger, they excelled at detecting when my patience was a pretended patience. You know the kind – it oozes insincerity. They made it very clear to me that if I was just using a technique rather than really listening, it wasn't going to work. I learned to admit when I didn't have patience for something and ask for cooperation rather than pretending to be patient.

For instance, when I was writing the first edition of this book, I let everyone know that I needed to concentrate for the next hour and had very little patience for being interrupted. This is part of limit setting, letting people who live with you know what they can expect from you.

When my children were young, I liked using the expression used in *How To Talk So Kids Will Listen And Listen So Kids Will Talk* to describe my patience - "It's as big as a watermelon," or "It's as small as a pea and shrinking." When I am rushed because I have been on the run all day my patience is "as small as a pea." This is not the time I invite anyone into the kitchen to help me make a meal.

When my children were younger and were cooking or baking, I sometimes left the kitchen because all I saw was the mess being made rather than the food that was being created. Unless I knew I could be present with patience, I didn't start an activity with my children that required presence and patience. Of course there were many times when my children required my presence and patience and I had to find the patience required. Breathing and looking into their eyes helped.

I am sure that most of us carry an image around in our heads of "the perfect mother." Mine is someone who never loses her temper, makes cookies with her children and doesn't get frustrated by the mess, keeps the house spotless, reads and plays games with her children, is always available, never wants time to herself, and has oodles of patience. Part of my learning patience has consisted of my tackling this impossible model I carry around with me. I lose patience with myself for not being this "perfect" woman. Humor often restores my perspective. So does breathing. I find it helpful to breathe deeply three or four times when I am at the edge, and during that time to imagine myself a tree with roots growing down deep into the ground, and sunlight coming through my leaves.

Breastfeeding my children helped me to learn to do this slowing down. One of the great gifts that breastfeeding provides a mother is that as you nurse you need to sit. As the baby nurses, a hormone (prolactin) is released that has a calming affect. I learned, while nursing each of my four children, how important it was to slow down and look them in the eyes and be reminded of just what mothering is all about. When I would look one of my children in the eyes, I was refreshed by the love that we shared, I became reconnected to my child, and my patience was often restored. I found that there was a shift in my perception.

Since my last baby weaned, I have had to consciously decide to relax instead of relying on a hormone to do it for me. I am glad I had as many years of nursing babies/toddlers as I did, so that I could learn how effective this slowing down is for my ability to be patient and keep things in perspective.

It is so easy to get caught up and move at a fast nonstop pace. However, sometimes slowing down, slowing the pace inside ourselves gives us more room to maneuver. Let me give you an example. When Josh plays the harp, he is often playing notes in very rapid succession. He never looks hurried, his hands stay relaxed and he takes all the time allotted to play the notes. There is no sense of hurry even when he is moving rapidly. Instead, there is a sense of grace, of being in the present. I try to keep this in mind when I am late getting to somewhere I need to go. My being in a rush inside my head isn't going to get me there any faster.

11. Be willing to develop observational skills

In order to help a child learn something, it is vital that you know the child. The difference for me between teaching my children at home and teaching in a school setting was that I had the opportunity to observe my children. Teachers in school settings also learn about children by observation, but very few of them have the opportunity for the almost unlimited time and access that a home-schooling mother can have. In the process of observing my children, I learned how differently they all acquire knowledge. What works for one child has not necessarily worked for another.

When they were younger, I played with them with blocks, Lego, dolls, cars and trucks, puzzles, etc. This play time helped me to see how they processed information. I used opportunities as they arose to present a new idea to a child or to suggest a different approach to accomplish whatever was being played with. The years I spent observing my children helped me to be sensitive to their own particular learning styles. I found it fascinating to note their differences and similarities.

As I worked with my children on something like reading, I continually monitored their feelings. If they were having fun and enjoying themselves, we continued. If they were barely tolerant, we set a time limit and stuck to it. I sometimes said, "It looks to me as though you are really enjoying this." I made my observations available to them. They gave me feedback as well by telling me about their feelings and perceptions as we worked together. In this way, I modeled the importance of observation, of being in touch with oneself, while doing something.

One of the ways we learn about how the world functions is by observing and drawing conclusions and then testing them - a scientific approach to life. The greater our ability to observe, to increase our vision, the wider our understanding can be. Observing my children has been one of my greatest joys. It was a great privilege to be able to observe how they learned and to find ways to support their learning. In the process, I made mistakes, lost my patience, and learned a lot about my own learning style.

12. Be willing to change

All the characteristics I have listed up to now, point the way to this last one - a willingness to change, to being flexible and responsive. Living with children means living with constant change as they are always growing and changing. The ideas I had about homeschooling when I started deepened and changed over the years. I had to let go of some assumptions and hold firm to others.

Sometimes, change can be devastating; sometimes, it can be exhilarating. Sometimes, it can be both. Whatever emotion we use to describe change, it is inevitable. It is a natural part of life; it defines life. One of the best things about being a homeschooling mother is that you are an active part of the changes your children experience as they grow. Being involved with so much change and growth, you can't help but grow and change as well.

Josh and Noah

CHAPTER 2
Creating A Learning Environment

The importance of play

Encouraging positive social interaction

A list of equipment, materials, and toys that facilitate play

Environment - *The New Lexicon Webster's Encyclopedic Dictionary of The English Language (Canadian Edition),* defines it as "surroundings, especially the material and spiritual influences which affect the growth, the development and existence of a living being." Create is defined as "to bring into being." When we homeschool, we need to bring into being material and spiritual influences that will support and encourage a child to gain mastery of the skills needed to function in the world. This is a pretty big order! It may look kind of scary, and yet we have been doing this since our children were born.

In this chapter, I want to share with you some of my ideas about how to create a learning environment conducive to homeschooling. Please keep in mind that each family will create their own unique environment; one that fits their needs. At the same time as each family will have a unique learning environment, there are some things that I think are important to include in all homeschooling learning environments. First and foremost for successful homeschooling is that children need to have a place to play and things to play with. Play is the "work" of childhood!

The Importance Of Play

The picture book, *How Tom Beat Captain Najork and His Hired Sportsmen* by Russell Hoban, seems to me to capture the essence of homeschooling in quite a delightful way. Tom just "messes" around and doesn't seem to do any sort of studying. This bothers his aunt who decides to show Tom how foolish this is. She invites Captain Najork to compete against Tom hoping to demonstrate to Tom that he needs to spend time with more formal studies. Tom wins all the contests because he has "fooled around" with all sorts of things and is better able than the sportsmen to play the games.

Children need to play and fool around with things; it's an important part of learning. We in our North American culture have formalized learning to such a great extent (classes for toddlers and preschoolers on how to do everything from singing to working a computer), that it may be difficult to accept that the time children spend "messing around" has any value whatsoever much less an educational value. Yet play, non-adult directed play, is vital to a child's intellectual growth and creative abilities. In order for us to understand things, we need to have a primary experience of what we are trying to understand. We need something to hang our experience on. *La experiencia es la madre de la ciencia. Experience is the mother of knowledge.* Cervantes

The book, *Truckers* by Terry Pratchett about some nomes (this is how Pratchett spells this word) illustrates this point. Most of the nomes have lived inside a store building for many generations and cannot even conceive that anything outside the store exists; that there is an "outside." When a group of nomes come to the store who have lived "outside," it takes a long time for the store nomes to believe in the existence of this other kind of life which is another world to them. To then learn that all nomes came from a star and were travelling through space when they landed on the earth is beyond the comprehension of most of the store nomes. As they have only experienced life in the store, they cannot even conceive of "outside" much less other planets or stars.

Play gives children primary experience to draw on as they get older. A child learns about numbers and the one to one correspondence of numbers as he plays with Lego blocks, dolls, or other toys. A child who has not had experience manipulating objects and not been allowed time to observe the relationships of objects - i.e., that three objects are three objects no matter how they are arranged cannot understand the concepts of arithmetic. A child who has not experienced moving his body through space will have a hard time understanding gravity and velocity.

During play, children also integrate their experiences with the knowledge they have acquired and test out how the things they have heard or learned about actually work. Play provides children with opportunities to try things out. Building with Lego, blocks or tinker toys gives children a sense of how gravity works with small objects. Swinging, jumping rope, riding a bicycle, or riding on a merry-go-round are some ways to learn about gravity with the whole body. Learning with the body - somatic learning - is something that is basic to understanding. Children need many experiences with natural forces or objects so that they have a framework to later understand the intellectual concepts that describe the natural forces at work on our planet. Play - inside and out of doors, imaginary, mentally or physically active - is vital to a child's developing intellectual powers and creative abilities.

Vivian Gussin Paley in her book *A Child's Work: The Importance of Fantasy Play* discusses at length the importance and value of fantasy play for children. She taught kindergarten for 35 years.

She's written a number of books about children and play. Here's a quote from Chapter 20:

> Every day brought me new evidence of the preeminence of fantasy in children's thinking. It has reinforced my certainty that we perform a grave error when we remove fantasy play as the foundation of early childhood education.
>
> We are going too far in the opposite direction. Some school people feel that because young children engage in magical thinking we must pull them on to another track as early as possible; having added extra years of schooling to their lives, we are emboldened to counteract fantasy play with "reality-based" activities.
>
> Is this not the adult version of magical thinking? To imagine that the purpose of early childhood education is to reorder the stages of human development is like the story of the prince who was turned into a frog. In attempting to turn children into creatures who are unchildlike, we ignore all the messages young children give us as they play. The frog turns back into a prince when the princess recognizes his need to be treated with kindness and respect. In the case of our children, this would include the kindness of acknowledging that their perceptions and premises are not the same as older children's or as our own.

Clarisa Pinkola Estes, in her book *Women Who Run With The Wolves* discusses the importance of play in creative life. Play allows us to experience things for their own sakes, to see what will happen if this and that are put together or this and that are put here under this. Play leads to new discoveries not only for children but for adults as well.

I found it fascinating to see the sorts of things my children did as they played. When the oldest two boys, Josh and Noah were young (5 through 8 years old) among the many other things that they did, they loved playing with little cars. They spent hours racing them and kept track of which car was the fastest in which situation - statistics. Robin and Holly at that age played with families of little animals, Lego people, or stuffed animals - sociology. As Robin grew older, he, like his older brothers, played more statistically oriented games. It is only our formal educational system that divides the world into various subject categories. In life, as in play, there are no divisions. One thing leads to another, and children discover facets of the world that do not fall into neat and tidy categories as they play.

Children play in all sorts of ways and in all sorts of physical environments. I have seen little girls play in the shoe department of K-Mart, while their mom was shopping for shoes, creating an entire world within the space of a few minutes. Play is as natural and as necessary for children as breathing. Let's look at some of the things you can do to support and encourage your children in their play.

Creating Space to Play

Some families limit children's play to certain rooms in the house. Some families have no limit to where the play takes place as long as it doesn't endanger anyone. You need to find what feels comfortable for your family. I found that when my children were young, they liked to play close to where I was. As they grew older, they wanted more private personal space in addition to our common family space.

There are two main factors to consider when creating play space for children:
1. safety - both physical and emotional
2. materials

Physical Safety

Physical safety can be challenging when there are children of varying ages in a household. Small toddlers and babies do not understand why they cannot put small Lego pieces in their mouths or that certain block structures are not meant for them to knock down. When I had both babies and older children, I established certain safety precautions for both the babies and the older children. It is important for a baby not to be endangered by small objects within his grasp. It is equally important for older children to know that their creations will not be destroyed.

We kept things like little Lego pieces in the older children's bedroom. The door was kept closed so that their creations were safe, and the babies were kept safe from swallowing things. This was OK for the younger children when they were babies. As they grew older, they wanted to be part of whatever was going on and began to express a desire to play with similar toys. This presented a challenge and required a lot of supervision on my part to ensure the younger child's safety, i.e., that he or she didn't swallow the small pieces.

Keeping play spaces safe for varying ages means that you need to do a lot of supervising. A 6 year old cannot always remember to pick up little objects that may be harmful for a crawling baby. It is important to state the expectations of the family - small objects need to be where babies can't reach them - and then help a child to follow this expectation. Setting up a separate play space for older children as I did can make it easier for this expectation to be carried out. Small objects can then be kept in private play space rather than in communal play space.

Safety issues can be a challenge. It means anticipating and thinking ahead. It also means supervising play. It is a great challenge to provide room for children's expression without compromising their physical safety.

Let me give you an example. My boys were always fascinated with sticks. When they were under 5, the rule was that sticks were never used in "pretend" fights. They just did not have the physical or emotional control to avoid hurting someone. As they grew older, we would have long drawn out discussions regarding the safety rules involved in "pretend" fighting using these sticks as swords. We finally agreed that they could fight with "real" stick swords against imaginary people. No matter how careful they would be, someone would get hurt if they were "pretend" fighting with each other. Neither one of them liked being hurt or hurting the other. Sometimes the one who was hurt would get so angry at being hurt that he would lose control and, instead of playing, begin to fight in earnest. Fighting pretend people was not very satisfactory, and we would start the discussion all over again and come up with new solutions such as using foam swords or other soft objects.

As you can see from this example, we tried to find a solution that would fit the need for the boys to play without injury and their desire to play in a satisfying manner. We constantly revised and discussed how to do this.

There were some things that I was not willing to compromise on such as safety equipment: bike helmets when riding a bike; wrist, knee, and elbow guards and a helmet when roller blading; baseball helmets and athletic supporters when playing baseball; helmets when horseback riding; seatbelts when traveling in the car; etc.

The model you set for safety in your home shows your child that you are serious about safety. At the same time that you provide safety equipment/protection, you need to be aware that there are no guarantees that a child will not get hurt. We risk being hurt when we are actively engaged in living. Your job as a homeschooling mother is to provide as safe an environment as you can.

My children have had stitches; been knocked unconscious from falls; suffered sprained ankles and wrists; bruises; and cuts. These are part and parcel of playing, exploring, learning. In the process of learning, we have become more aware of certain safety hazards, and found ways to prevent further accidents of the same nature. There is no "perfect" environment where children can play risk free. Because as homeschooling mothers we have children in our care for many more hours than most mothers do, it is vital to provide as safe a physical environment as we can.

Emotional Safety

As well as physical safety, we need to provide emotionally safe places for our children. We need to give clear guidelines to our children about how to appropriately express their feelings. Homeschooling, if you have more than one child, means that your children will be together each and every day. People have often asked me how I could cope - their own children fought so much of the time when they were home together. How did I manage with my children home all the time?

Because homeschooling siblings are with each other many hours of the day, the issues of how siblings relate to each other have to be addressed. There is no escape. The family value system needs to be defined. What is acceptable behavior needs to be clearly and constantly stated so that children can learn appropriate ways of expressing themselves. This is hard work. Limit setting - when you stick to the choices you have made about the tone, the atmosphere of your family environment - means hours of introspection, hours of discussion (both heated and calm between you and your children and your spouse or partner), and hours of self-doubt as you try to establish an atmosphere of respect and consideration.

In order to come to a clear picture of what defines a safe place - a place where children are protected from harm, both physical and emotional; a place where children are encouraged and supported in their endeavors - you will struggle to consciously define your value system. Sometimes parents who decide to homeschool in reaction to the strictness and lack of responsiveness of formalized public schooling throw out not only requirements for how to go about learning but also requirements about how to relate to others - the "anything goes" philosophy that says that children will sort out for themselves how to relate to others if just given a free rein. I have seen too much harm that comes from this approach. It looks to me like a way to chaos rather than a way to help children learn how to relate to each other. I knew in my heart from years of being with children both before becoming a mother and since that in order for children to learn, they need to be safe.

To create a safe emotional place for children to play in our family we had these three rules.

1. No hitting, pinching, etc.

2. No name calling

3. Each person and his/her belongings needs to be treated with respect

Restraining children when they are angry and expressing their anger with violence toward others is difficult. It was difficult for me because I had to work hard to learn to use something other than violence (spanking) when I went over the edge in anger or frustration by my children's behavior. As a culture, we have become more aware of the pervasiveness of violence. We find it reprehensible in many situations, yet we have not resolved our fascination with violence as a solution to a problem nor realized how deeply violent behavior is ingrained in our culture. Spanking a child is still considered by many to be an acceptable parenting tool.

I worked hard to learn how to set limits and stick to those limits instead of finding myself frustrated to the point of spanking because my children were not doing as I asked. I was motivated to do this hard work because it was clear to me that if I expected my children to not hit or hurt others when they were angry, I couldn't either.

Spanking a child is a signal for parents to find ways to increase their repertoire of parenting skills. Hitting is a simplistic way of solving a problem. It doesn't really solve the problem. It changes it and defines who is stronger and more powerful. The problem is still there. The problem may be a battle between a child's needs or wants and an adult's needs or wants. Spanking resolves the problem of who should get what by making it clear that the person with the most physical power is right. This is not a message I wanted to send to my children.

Becoming a more effective parent is such a big topic, that many books have been written about it and about how to break the cycle of violence administered to children in the name of discipline. The article *Spanking: A Shortcut to Nowhere* by Penelope Leach is well written and helpful. The site www.nospank.net has information about various states in the US that have enacted no spanking laws. I have listed books that I found particularly helpful in the bibliography. I won't go on at length here about spanking, but just mention a few things that helped me to change.

Please remember as you work to help yourself, your child, or children to find solutions to problems that do not include violence that you are doing something that is difficult, valuable and powerful. It is only by each individual making choices that do not include violence, that change will come. If you give your children tools and examples of how to solve problems without using violence, you are giving them a gift. You also give a gift to our whole planet. We desperately need a new way of looking at how we solve problems on our planet. There is no more "them" and "us." (There never has been.) We all breathe the same air, drink the same water and live on the same planet. We live in a large family - the earth's family. The work you do to help your family/your children to find ways to solve problems that treat each person with respect will have many positive repercussions.

By the time my third and fourth children came along, I had learned how to set limits without using spanking. I never spanked very often, but I wish I could say I had not done it at all. My earnest desire to change and my commitment to finding a new "language" of mothering skills made it possible for me to learn how to state my expectations. At the same time, I learned to accept, not just intellectually understand, that children are children and will need help to do those things they are asked to do.

I learned to really take the time it takes to count to ten before acting on any aggressive impulse. I learned to walk away if I couldn't cope. I learned that raising small children and being with them 24 hours a day was a stressful job and required all that I had - all the way down to the ends of my toes and beyond. I learned to look into my children's eyes and see the child and not the act that was driving me over the edge. I was fortunate. The cycle of violence I inherited was not an overwhelming one. I could stop. The material I quoted in the first chapter about forgiveness from *Mastering Your Hidden Self* by Serge King was very useful to me as I looked back and wished I had stopped spanking earlier.

Name-calling or verbal abuse is another form of violence that pervades our society. It may seem less destructive than physical violence but it's effects are just as damaging as physical violence. That's why I set the limit of no name-calling or verbal abuse. This did not mean that my children did not have angry feelings or yell at each other. It meant that when they were angry I helped them to find acceptable ways to express that anger - using words to describe their feelings, hitting a pillow instead of a brother, going outside and screaming, etc. We all learned together as they grew older and were more able to express themselves verbally rather than physically.

In the early years, I often felt that being a mother meant being a fireman putting out the fires of arguments and fury. Sometimes, I got caught up in the blaze and fanned the flames rather than putting out the fire. My learning curve of motherhood was often greater than I would have liked.

Let me give you an example of limit-setting. When I only had the three boys, some neighborhood boys came to play with Josh and Noah. The four boys played outside and had fun for a while. Then the neighbors started suggesting that they play some sort of game that involved teasing Robin. I was outside working in the garden and keeping an eye on Robin because he was only 18 months old at the time. He went from playing with a hose, being with me, to following his older brothers around. After the game was suggested, I could see that Josh and Noah were uncomfortable. They were 7 and 5 years old at the time. I intervened and said "The rules at our house are that if you play with someone, you do not pick on them or attack them. I can't let you play the kind of game you suggested." The neighbors decided to go home, and after a few more visits, by mutual decision, they no longer came to play.

Some people think that children need to sort this out for themselves and would find my intervention interference. I think that children need help to know what family values are as well as help to uphold those family values until such a time as they can be their own advocates. Their ability to do this happens as they grow older. I think it asks a lot of a 7 year old to be able to verbalize a family limit and uphold it without parental support.

Various people expressed concern to me that because I provided such a protected atmosphere, my children wouldn't learn how to assert and stand up for themselves as they grew older. The overprotection of children is a topic of concern in 2007. It is a confusing topic. It's easy to confuse protection with stifling. Children need to be able to play and to direct their play at the same time we as parents need to protect the environment in which they play. Finding the balance between the two is a constantly changing one. We are confused by the media about the dangers that are ever present for children at the same time that we wish to give them the opportunity to explore the world. Children think that the reasons we don't allow them to go to the park on their own when they are 8 years old is because we don't trust them. When in reality we don't trust that the park is a safe place for our child to be on his own because there are other people who are not safe.

Here's an incident that happened in a public park one summer day. At the beach, Robin (11), Holly (8), and their friend (11) were playing in the water. Near to where they were swimming, a man, who was drunk, was splashing water at a number of children. I was on the beach. I thought that as this man began to splash my children, that they were OK with this. Then I really noticed the looks on their faces and got up, ready to intervene. At the same time, Robin stood and faced the man and told him to stop throwing the water. Josh (17) had come closer on his air mattress and called the attention of the lifeguard to this man. Holly, crying, ran out of the water to me. The man responded with some nasty words. I said something to him and took Holly away from the water. The lifeguard came and told the man he needed to go sit on the beach for a while. Robin ran out of the water, and began to cry. Josh came up and we all talked about it.

I apologized to Holly and Robin that I hadn't done something to stop this man earlier. At the same time, I told Robin that I
was proud of the way he had stood up for his sister, his friend and
himself in such an assertive way. He acted on his knowledge that
he did not need to accept this man's behavior.

It didn't surprise me that Josh did what he did, but it really
surprised me that Robin did. He was only 11 years old and he acted
to defend himself, his sister and his friend. He was willing to risk
this man's wrath to stand up for himself and his sister and friend.
Robin knew that I was on the beach but I hadn't yet done anything
to help.

There were lots of adults on the beach watching this man
and his buddy drinking beer, which is illegal in any public park in
the municipality where we live, throwing water at children. None
of us had acted to stop this man. Robin had the courage to face
him and tell him to leave him alone.

This incident demonstrated that Robin knew that he had
the power to change this situation. It demonstrated to me that I
had not disabled my children's ability to assert themselves. I realized afterwards that no matter how one tries to create a safe play
space, one free of emotional and physical abuse or hazards, life is
not without risk. We cannot make our children's lives risk free. As
children grow older, they'll reach out to the world in all kinds of
ways. We cannot prevent hurt, anguish, betrayal, and/or pain. We
can be there beside them when this occurs, validating their negative
feelings as well as their positive ones and support them as they
come to grips with less than ideal situations.

I felt that my job as a mother was to find a way to support
my children in their reaching out while at the same time making it
as safe as possible. I weighed the risks associated with an activity
and tried to decide if the benefits outweigh the costs. This skill
takes time and experience to master. It is a skill children must learn

if they are to survive.

Robin and Holly took horseback riding lessons. Horseback riding can be dangerous, so I looked for a teacher whose judgment I could trust. The teacher I found was someone I felt very comfortable with. I appreciated the way he worked with my children. He was aware of their limitations and never suggested that they try something unless he thought they could do it. He did not want to see them or the horses get hurt anymore than I did. If their teacher had pushed them beyond what I thought was reasonable, I would not have hesitated to speak up.

When my children have taken lessons in sports such as riding or gymnastics, I sat in on their lessons. It helped me to get a better sense of how a teacher worked with my children. I also made a point to ask my children how they felt about their lessons and their teachers. I wanted them to know that if they were uncomfortable with a teacher or situation or feeling unhappy but not able to pinpoint why that I would help them make a change.

I sat on the sidelines. I didn't interfere with the class but was there watching. My children were there to learn things from this instructor because the instructor had skills my children wanted to learn. There's a fine line between being there to support one's child and being there to micromanage. It helped me to think about how I would feel if I were the instructor; what would make me feel as though this person supported her child as well as the lessons being imparted.

It's important for a child to feel that a parent is still involved and on his side when learning outside of the family - that mom will make it safe. As my children grew older, they didn't need my actual physical presence whenever they participated in an activity outside of the family. However, they still enjoyed my willingness to watch them in their activities and needed me to be interested and aware of what they were doing.

As well as ensuring that a teacher is aware of physical safety, we need to be aware of the potential of other kinds of harm a child may suffer. I mention this because it is important to be aware that not all adults who work with children are "safe." We send out a lot of very mixed messages to children in our society. On the one hand, we warn them not to talk to strangers. On the other hand, many children have been raised by strangers since they were small by being placed in daycare centers. Or children go to classes and are expected to listen to and follow the instruction of these strangers. How can a child discriminate between a stranger who is OK and a stranger who is not?

Homeschooling gave me a great advantage in ensuring safety for my children, because they had me there to protect them. As they grew older, they reached out on their own, no longer needing me to be present, but still consulting me when they needed help to sort out what constitutes a safe, positive environment. Older teens and those in their early twenties still need this kind of emotional support. Actually, we all need this kind of support whether from good friends, partners, or support groups. Make sure that as your children grow older that they know that you are still there to listen and support them in their judgments about people or situations. Children have been sexually and emotionally abused in sports, music, and other recreational programs. Stay in touch with your child and his or her teachers, coaches, instructors. Monitor how your child is feeling about his or her activities outside the home.

Creating a positive and safe emotional environment has been one of the most rewarding parts of homeschooling for me. It has not come easily. I labored to create a safe atmosphere for my children. I felt terribly isolated and alone at times. I often wondered if I was doing the right thing. Now that my children are adults, I have no doubt that the work I did to create a warm, loving, supportive, safe and creative atmosphere paid off. The energy I used to "fill their tanks" with unconditional love by giving them my attention has been returned many times over.

Finding Someone to Play With - Social Interaction

At the present time in our society, we have come to believe that children do best in large groups of children of similar ages. I question if this is actually beneficial for children. As a species, we do not have babies in litters. Twins and triplets are the exception, singletons the rule when we give birth. I have an instinctive feeling that children do better in smaller groups than larger groups and that they need the presence of adults to help them learn how to relate to others.

Children do a lot of learning by observation and mimicry. A group with various ages such as a family, gives children an opportunity to observe how people of various ages relate to others as well as being able to help each other with learning tasks.

Before arranging a social life for your homeschooled child, take time to think about just how much interaction with other children is necessary and/or valuable. Some children thrive on being with others, some fade with too much social interaction, and some are a mix of both. Take time to discover how much social interaction works well for your child. When my children were young and had a particularly good time with friends, they wanted to do it again the next day. Sometimes this worked, but often it didn't. Too much of a good thing, like a steady diet of chocolate cake, doesn't nourish even though it might taste good at first.

Children need time to be at home to have time to themselves. They need time to digest the experiences they have had. Mothers need time with children to be in touch with what they are thinking, experiencing, and learning.

My children had each other to play with. When they were young, they developed ongoing games that they played both inside and out. They still enjoy playing with each other now that they're adults. They're not all together often, but when they are, playing games is still a part of how they spend their time together. They developed close and satisfying relationships with each other as children that have continued into their adult lives.

Siblings provide convenient playmates. One of the benefits of homeschooling is that as siblings grow older, they can continue to play together and develop their relationship. When a child goes to school, he may no longer be interested in being "friends" with his younger brothers or sisters. Social interaction is focused on age peers. This can be quite devastating for a younger sibling who has just begun to be able to play well with an older sibling. Homeschooled siblings often provide each other with companionship and friendship that is rare for schooled siblings.

Second in terms of convenience and accessibility are neighborhood children. It may be that you live in a neighborhood where children play outside and your child can join in. Some homeschoolers have found this works well. Others have found that their homeschooled child is singled out for some teasing and razing because of the way he is educated.

Learning how to relate to others is a skill that is developed over time, like any other skill such as reading. When your child is playing with another child, he learns how to be with other children, what makes him happy when he is with others, and what makes him unhappy. You can provide safety for your child by being there and letting him know that he is welcome to come and be with you if he is uncomfortable or unsure. You can help your child by sharing your observations with him. If you see that your son is hesitant to go and play with other children on a playground, you could say "I saw that you were standing and watching the children play at the park today." Your son may answer with a monosyllable or tell you how he was feeling. You can continue the conversation and give him words for what you think he might have felt if you think it is appropriate. "When I saw you looking at them, I wondered if you felt afraid/shy/hesitant to join them?"

Giving your child an opportunity to reflect on his experience and feelings allows him to better know himself. Respect your child's pace in making social contacts and offer your help but don't push him into a situation he is not ready for. "Is there a way I can help you when we are at the playground?" Your support and encouragement helps your child learn about himself and his social experiences.

Some children like being in groups. Finding groups of children may prove a challenge if you are homeschooling or it may not depending on where you live. In many communities there are homeschooling classes, field trips, and/or events for both parents and children. In fact, some families who homeschool in such an environment find that they need to make sure they actually have some time at home.

As well as siblings and neighborhood children, there are recreation center classes that can provide group interaction for a homeschooled child. Other avenues to explore are scouting, guiding, sports teams, church groups, or other group activities organized for children in your community. Sometimes group activities that worked for your child at one age may no longer be interesting to your child at a different age. Some homeschooled children have been welcomed into the nonacademic parts of a neighborhood school such as drama productions, band, orchestra, or sports teams. This may be something to explore especially if you live in a rural area. This can be a way for your child to make friends with children who attend school.

Observe your children and how they are responding to social interaction as you set up ways of meeting your children's social needs. Monitor their behavior and general state. Sometimes, when a child is playing with others in a group, he or she may be O.K. at the time, but once he or she is at home unhappiness, anger, sadness may be expressed. This is a time to talk and discuss what happened. Your child may not be able or willing to share his feelings right after something happens. Bedtime is often a good time to go over the events of the day. It's dark; there's a more relaxed atmosphere making it easier for a child to share his feelings.

Remember as you help your child find playmates that it takes time to develop friendships. Friendship is often easier if the people involved have similar interests and/or backgrounds. Many homeschooling children have found it easier to be friends with other homeschooling children. To go about finding other homeschooling families, check your local library for information about homeschooling support groups. If there is no such group in your community, you may wish to put up signs in public places announcing your interest in meeting with others interested in homeschooling.

What I am suggesting here is what I suggested in the first chapter - find or create a support network or system, and perhaps you will find children who enjoy playing with your children and vice versa. Keep in mind however that just because children are homeschooled doesn't mean that they will enjoy each other's company, but it can be a place to start.

When meeting with another homeschooling family (or any other family) for the first time, it may be easier for everyone, if you meet in neutral territory, say a park. That way, if the children do not "click," there is less of an obligation. It can be easier for children to begin a friendship in a neutral territory especially when they are younger. In a park or at the beach, the equipment is public and doesn't belong to any of the children or families. Meeting in this neutral territory allows both families to assess if a friendship is possible.

Remember that even children attending school do not always find friends. They have classmates and acquaintances, but many children attending school feel pleased if they have one close friend.

You are also a playmate for your child. The games that you play with your child are a valuable part of homeschooling. Your child needs your attention and willingness to participate in her life as much as she needs friends who are children.

One of the things that I've noticed about homeschooled children is that they are able to cross age and gender boundaries when they play. They are able to play with children of varying ages, based on whether or not the children in question enjoy each other's company rather than whether they are the same age. My older boys played basketball, soccer, and baseball with Robin and his friend, Robert. Holly was included when she wanted to be. These four boys of varying ages had a good time together playing physically active games as well as more quiet games such as "Magic." For many homeschooling children, interest and compatibility determine their choice of friends rather than age or gender.

Adult life consists of relationships that are not limited to age peers and instead are more related to interest. Homeschooled children have a distinct advantage over schooled children in that they have the opportunity to experience relationships with people of all ages because they are not in school for six hours a day.

I referred earlier to my children playing together and being each other's friends. I do not mean to imply that homeschooling your children will automatically ensure that they enjoy playing with each other. You need to facilitate the possibility of their play by making sure they have time together and establishing guidelines to ensure that their play is "safe" as I mentioned at the beginning of this chapter. You may have children whose interests and tempera-ments are dissimilar. This makes creating a peaceful home a chal-lenge. To create a home where the members of a family support and basically like each other is something worth working toward, even though it often requires more effort than you were expecting to give.

As I said earlier, it is important to take time to think about just what kind and how much social interaction with others outside the family you choose to have. It may be that seeing other children once a week is about all your 6 year old can cope with. That's perfectly normal. Some children do not enjoy being around other children very much. Other children thrive. You need to observe your child and your family and find what works best for all of you. You may not find a "best" friend for your child. It may prove difficult to find other children in your vicinity with whom your child "clicks." This also happens to children attending school and is not directly related to homeschooling. As long as your child has some people he talks with, relates to, plays games with, he will have an opportunity to learn about relationships. That's what socialization is all about.

Toys, Materials and Equipment

Before I begin this list of toys, materials, and equipment let me just say a few words about the value of having time to play outside in the natural world. My mom used to say to me frequently that "If you give children sand and water, they will always find something to do with it and be happy." I remember going to the beach when we lived in Holland, a 45 minute walk from our apartment. My mom pushed us in a buggy, carried us on her bike, or, as I got older, helped me to scoot along on a scooter while she pushed my younger brother and sister in a buggy. (I have a brother who is 2½ years younger than I am and a sister who is 4½ years younger.) I can still remember being in the dunes, then going and playing on the beach, jumping in the waves. When it was too cold for the beach, she took us to a wooded park that involved a similar walk.

We went to either the beach or the forest everyday unless the weather was really awful.

After we moved to the U.S. when I was 8 years old, we still lived in an apartment with no yard, but there was a vacant lot next door where I would sometimes play, as well as a wooden porch over a set of garages. I had friends with yards where I played. My mom still took us to parks, walking there with us. She began working because my father could not find steady work. On the weekend, we went to parks, lakes or an arboretum so that we could play outside in the natural world.

My father died when he was 44. My mom was 41 at the time and had three children 13, 11, and 9. She had to keep working to support us. Now that I am much older than my mother was when my father died, I have even more admiration for the decisions she made. She continued to take us to beaches, pools, the arboretum, and parks in the evenings, on week days and on the weekends even though there were many household tasks that needed doing. She gave me two gifts: a connection with the earth and the natural world that I am thankful for everyday, and her presence as we played in the natural world. She made it clear that she valued us - our childhood and our need for time to play and have fun while she was with us, watching or participating.

So go out with your child into the rain, the wind, the storms, and the night as well as out on the sunny days. Even if you live in an apartment in a city, there are parks and bits of green that can give a child an experience with forces other than man-made ones. I think this is vital for children's well being. Richard Louv author of *Last Child In The Woods: Saving our Children From Nature-Deficit Disorder* writes, "Healing the broken bond between our young and nature is in our self-interest, not only because aesthetics or justice demand it, but also because our mental, physical, and spiritual health depend upon it." You can read more about the movement he has started at: www.thefuturesedge.com

Let's move on now to the toys, equipment, and materials that will help you create a stimulating learning environment. Let's start with books and a library card. Although I will write more about books in Chapter 3 and 6, I want to stress here the value of libraries. If you live in a rural area, bookmobiles may provide the services of a library. If that is not possible, there may be mail order library services available through a university near you. Whatever it takes, it is worth your while, no matter how small the library, to try to find access to one. What better deal can there be than a library card? The whole world of books available to you free or at nominal cost.

Now don't you wish there were libraries for toys as well? In some cities there are. In fact in some libraries, games and puzzles are available for check out along with books. In other places, parents have started toy libraries. Toy libraries usually require a subscription fee in order to join. Members often work cooperatively to manage the exchange of the toys. Toy libraries can provide things like Brio train sets without individual families spending hundreds of dollars to purchase a complete set. Toy libraries can also give you a chance to see what kind of toys have staying power for your child. Sometimes children are desperately anxious to have a toy and find out a week later that this toy is not really as thrilling or exciting as it seemed at first.

How does one go about finding the toys and other materials that will last for more than a week if there is no toy lending library available? I wish I had the answer. I don't. I do have some suggestions for basic toys that seem to work for most children some of the time. These are the ones that I will list. You will need to determine which toys suit your child or children, which ones fit your family budget, and which ones suit your family's value system.

When first reading this list, it may seem overwhelming and

costly. Remember that no individual family starts out with all of these things, they are acquired over time. Birthday and other holiday gifts are often a time when children receive some of the more expensive toys or equipment that they enjoy playing with. Not all the things I list are expensive, nor do they need to be purchased new. We found garage sales, thrift shops, and/or newspaper ads great places to find secondhand toys and equipment.

It is important for homeschooling children to have a variety of things to play with. They will spend many hours at home, playing with the things you provide. You need to provide a full, diverse, and rich environment for learning if you intend to homeschool because the early years of life profoundly influence creativity and intelligence. Scrimping on equipment, materials and toys is not a savings nor is it necessary to be independently wealthy to acquire these things. As I said above, thrift shops, garage sales, etc. are often filled with bargains such as board games, puzzles, dolls, trucks, etc.

Before going into the specifics of what toys I recommend, I'd like to suggest that you have family toys as well as toys that belong to individual children. Let me clarify. It is important for children to have their own things so that they have a choice about sharing. At the same time, it is important to have things that all the children in the family can play with. A set of wooden blocks is an example of a family toy. One child may be playing with it and not want his creation destroyed, yet he understands that these blocks belong to the whole family and will need to be shared with other children in the family at some future time.

My husband and I ran a nursery school before our children were born. The toys we had for this school as well as some of my husband's childhood toys became family toys. They were kept in common areas of our house so that they were accessible to our children and to visiting children. Having family toys meant that our children weren't expected to share their own toys with visiting children unless they chose to do so. This may seem strange as one of the things we want to help children learn to do is to share.

When a child owns something and can make decisions about whether or not to share his toy, his decision to share is genuine and not forced on him. Imagine for a moment that someone comes over to visit and assumes that just because she is a guest in your home, she can start using your kitchen cooking equipment or your sewing machine. It would feel like an invasion of your privacy and boundaries. Assuming that your children should share their toys or belongings with other children is similar. Children will learn generosity better by the ways in which their parents demonstrate generosity than by being told to share their toys. When purchasing toys, ask yourself, "Is this toy for a specific child that will become his own or is this toy something for the whole family?"

Here's an alphabetized list of equipment, materials, and toys that we have found to be an integral part of our learning environment. This list is not meant to be complete. I included toys that we have found to have "staying power." Please take time to observe what your child enjoys doing. The addition of a new toy or piece of equipment may open up a new direction for a child or support him in an interest. It's fun to find something that your child really enjoys. It's one of the delights of being a parent.

I have listed mainly big sorts of toys. There are lots of little toys - like magnifying glasses or marbles that can bring as much delight and pleasure to a child as an expensive set of Playmobile. What your child has to play with in part determines the kind of play that he engages in. The more you can do to support your child's interest, the more able your child is to pursue this interest. You let your child know that his play is important when you provide him with suitable material and toys to play with. And, as I said earlier in this chapter, play is very important for children. Toys are the tools of your homeschooling environment, necessary for your children to have so that they can develop their creative abilities.

Art and craft materials

Colored Pencils - My children liked to use these. They each had their own set of 60 colored pencils and we had a family set or two as well. I like the kind that comes in box that will stand up so that you can see all the colors.

Craft materials - beads, fabric scraps (if you don't sew, you could post a note at a local fabric store asking for scraps), popsicle sticks, feathers, buttons, sequins, dried pasta, ribbons, old jewelry, etc. A box of ribbons, lace, buttons, etc. makes a fun present.

Crayons - these did not get used very much at our house, but we have lots of them around. I can think of few things as satisfying as a new box of wax crayons! We used Neocolor II Aquarelle crayons by Caran D'Ache for face painting. These water soluble crayons wash off the face very easily. They are available in large and small boxes and often in individual colors. We use oil pastels and chalk pastels more frequently than wax crayons. They are bright and cover a lot of area very quickly.

Glue - Push up glue sticks are such a great invention! White liquid glue is good for some things, but we found that it is often just too slow for many projects. A glue gun with plastic glue sticks can be a very handy tool for older children. Beware because it's easy to burn fingers.

Modeling materials:

Bees Wax - Available in colored blocks specifically for modeling, soothing to work with, leaving hands soft and smelling like honey! It doesn't get hard even when exposed to air, requiring only requires the warmth of your hands to make it pliable. Even very young children can use it with ease.

Clay - satisfies an inborn need to mold and shape things.

Clay can be air dried or fired in a kiln or just put away to use another day. If there is a ceramics outlet nearby, you might ask them for suggestions about clay and firing it for more permanent creations . You may live somewhere near a place where you can dig clay out of the ground. Making things with clay can lead to all sorts of fascinating discussion about how people lived before there were stores.

Papier-Mâché - fun, messy, and recycles newspaper and other papers. Check your library for instruction books.

Plasticine - easily worked modeling material. We've used it when travelling. Each child had an individual package of thin strips of various colors of plasticine. Barbara Reid's illustrations in books like *The New Baby Calf* inspired us to create pictures with plasticine.

Playdough - either the commercial kind or the kind made at home (Google playdough recipes) is lots of fun. An inexpensive modeling material that like clay satisfies an urge to shape and mold. I found it a useful ice breaker for children just getting to know each other - lots of playdough at the kitchen table and various tools such as plastic spoons or metal spoons, canning jar lids, butter knives and a garlic press to shape it, cut it, or mold it. It's also soothing for moms to play with; squeezing it through the hands releases a lot of tension.

Sculpey - a modeling material that can be baked in a home oven to a hard finish. It's easy to use becoming pliable very quickly in your hand. My children used it to make decorations, earings, little toys and food for their Lego people, presents for their friends, etc. It doesn't stick to your hands and bakes fairly quickly, 10 -15 minutes at 250° F.   We like it better than Fimo which is a similar material but takes a lot longer to become pliable.

Paint - We used boxes of water color paints most frequently. (August is often a good month to buy these things as stores offer "Back to School" specials.) and large round blocks of water color. I found it very handy to have a big block of black to use to cover wax resist pictures. When Josh and Noah were little, I had an easel set up with jars of tempera paints available at all times. (If you mix a bit of soap powder with the powdered tempera and water, it washes out of clothes more readily.) They enjoyed this very much. Acrylic paints are fun to use as well. They give a satisfying finish to wooden objects.

Paper - I think it's vital to have lots of good quality (as good as you can afford) blank paper available for your children. Although it would seem ecologically sensible to use the backs of other papers, such as office paper or computer paper, once your child begins to express himself in recognizable ways on paper, you never know when he will create something special. It would be so sad if it were on the back of a flyer or an old letter. For this reason, we had lots of 8½" x 11" blank photocopy paper and larger sheets of paper available. If you are concerned about the volume of paper your children go through, use the backs of your children's rejected art work for lists, letters, etc. This art work (no longer wanted by your children) also makes great wrapping paper for gifts.

Sketchbooks are a way to keep drawings in one place. Check with art supply stores for inexpensive good quality paper. Let them know you are homeschooling, and ask if they'll give you a discount. These stores are also good places to get origami paper and other specialty papers.

Another source of paper is printers. Ask them if they give away their offcuts. They're a great source of all kinds of marvelous paper in odd sizes. Explain that you homeschool and need the offcuts for your schooling program.

Balls   We had lots of these in many sizes. Balls small enough to hold and throw easily; large balls with handles made especially to sit and bounce on; soft and squishy balls; hard balls; large, small, and medium size balls; and those tiny hard balls that bounce up ever so high. A can of new tennis balls was once a very welcome present for my boys not for tennis, but to play with. Nerf balls are great! My boys used the firm kind to play baseball with in our yard. We kept balls in boxes by the door and a few in the car. Balls are small fun toys. Spring is a great time to give a child a new ball to play with outside.

Bicycle   A bicycle gives a child wings. It's important to remember that if a child is going to ride a bike, he must like the bike - like the way it looks, feels, and handles. It's important for a child to under-stand what the limits of the family budget are, so that he knows what kind of bike it is possible for him to have. Sometimes getting a bike of a certain kind is so important to a child, that he is willing to earn money to contribute to the purchase. Once you have a bike for a child, make sure that child also has a proper helmet and wears it!

Blocks   Although wooden blocks are usually thought of as a toy for younger children, older children can and do enjoy building with blocks as well. Blocks were a family toy in our house. We often had the floor covered in block structures for various reasons: to create a place for little cars; to create farms for plastic farm animals; or to create houses for dolls.

It is important to have a set of blocks that match, i.e., they are half or twice as big as others and to have more than one of each shape and size. We found it fun to make blocks out of end cuts of lumber to add to a basic block set. Wooden and plastic spools and wooden beads are also good additions to a basic block set.

Cars, Trucks, and Other Vehicles Little "dinky" cars, tractors, big trucks, little trucks, new and used trucks are great toys for the imagination. Friction motor cars, cars that have sirens, trucks and tractors to be used in the sand add a lot to your child's play. These vehicles come in all sorts of price ranges. Garage sales or thrift stores often have good selections at very reasonable prices.

Dolls, Puppets, and Stuffed Animals Like balls, we had lots of these around the house. Our boys didn't play with dolls as much as Holly did, but they did play with stuffed animals, puppets, and little fuzzy plastic animals. All of these toys allow a child to be creative and engage in dramatic play.

When Josh and Noah were about 9 and 7, they made a number of finger puppets with felt and needle and thread. They put on plays with these as well as with our hand puppets. Each child also made a "Waldorf" type doll - a soft stuffed doll with a face that has just eyes and a straight line for a mouth. You can find instructions for making dolls and puppets online or at the library.

American Girl dolls are soft vinyl dolls with cloth bodies. You can see their wide selection of dolls - both baby and older dolls - online at www.americangirl.com. The dolls come in various skin tone shades, eye and hair color. They are childlike dolls. They make historical dolls as well as contemporary ones. The historical dolls have costumes and stories appropriate to their historical time. I have mixed feelings about all of their accessories for dolls, but I can see the appeal.

Dress-up Clothes Dress-up clothes of all kinds including lengths of cloth - shiny, filmy, bright, dark, patterned and plain - that can be fashioned into turbans, capes, skirts, belts, loin cloths, etc. are important to have. Garage sales, rummage sales, and/or thrift shops are good places to get things like fancy dresses, shoes, or wigs. Just before and right after Halloween is also a good time to acquire dress-up things such as masks, wigs, or face paint.

My children used our dress-up clothes to put on plays for us to watch or as they engaged in play themselves. It amazed me how they created costumes for different time periods from the same materials.

It's important to have a place to keep all of these things, so that they can be found again. Although I prefer to store things on shelves rather than in large boxes or bins, our dress-up trunk worked well. It always surprised me that everything fit back in and the lid closed after all the items had been taken out, sorted through, and used.

Games and Puzzles I will talk at length about games in Chapter 5, so please refer to that chapter for information about specific board and card games your family might enjoy. Games are an important part of a homeschooling curriculum. They provide children with opportunities to play within fixed boundaries.

Puzzles are a great way for a child to learn about patterns, matching shapes and colors, and spatial relationships. Start with simple puzzles. Once a child can do puzzles of 25 – 60 pieces, try ones with more pieces. We found 250 piece puzzles to be the most satisfying. They can be completed within a day but still present a challenge.

Lego As the Lego company says "It's a new toy everyday!" We have family Lego as well as individually owned Lego sets. It is such a creative toy - children can play with it in all sorts of imaginative ways while they learn about structure and form. I recommend getting three or four basic sets as a family starter set because it's important to have enough Lego pieces so that you can build more than one structure at a time. Then as needed and wanted, you can add more specialty sets for individual children or the family.

My boys played with Lego almost everyday even into their teens. There is something so appealing in how easily the pieces fit together. When they were younger and played with Lego everyday, we talked about how much fun it would be to go to Denmark to Lego-land to see a whole town made of Lego. We enjoyed looking at the pictures in the book *The World Of Lego Toys* by Henry Wieneck. It was fascinating to read how Lego was invented and developed and how Lego is used by both adults and children all over the world. Engineers and architects use Lego when making prototypes for buildings. There are even some colleges/universities who ask an applicant to build a Lego structure as part of their entrance requirement. It's a great toy!

Plastic animals add a lot to a child's creative play. As a child plays with these plastic animals, he can't help but absorb their details, the way they are formed. That's why it is important to have some animals that are anatomically correct and in proportion. It makes learning about animals just that little bit easier.

One of my favorite artists, Rien Poortvliet, in his book,

Noah's Ark, describes the large wooden toy boat - a Noah's ark - that his father made for him to use with his Britain plastic toy animals. Poortvliet's book is a compilation of his drawings of all the animals on planet earth with a very brief story line. It's beautiful. He must have absorbed the shape of many animals during his play.

Playmobile Two of my children enjoyed playing with Playmobile for many hours a day. They liked to play imaginative games and spent many hours having fun with this toy.

One of the things that is most charming about Playmobile is all the details - such as the little mittens and skates, etc. that come with the skaters. It can also be a drawback as a child has to spend time sorting out where all the small pieces are in order to play. Certainly a good way to learn organizational skills!

Some children like to keep their Playmobile in sets, ours was stored all together in a large plastic bin - sorted by category (adults, children, hats, small animals, etc.) in various smaller plastic containers or plastic bags. Sometimes you can find used Playmobile or Lego at garage sales or thrift stores. Whenever I found any, I felt that I'd struck gold as it is so expensive when new.

Sand Toys As I stated before making this list, playing with sand and water seems to bring joy to most children. A bucket and shovel are basics. You can add all sorts of other things to these: measuring cups, yogurt containers, sieves, molds, etc. There are lots of sand toys available. Get a bucket and shovel for yourself, too, and join your child to make things in the sand. See www.teamsandtastic.com for some amazing sand sculptures.

Sports Equipment I want to stress the need for providing equipment for big muscle activities. It's important for children to run about and move their bodies every day. Important for us, too. We had a Rebounder trampoline that provided us with hours of bog muscle activity during inclement weather. Equipment for games to play outside like badminton, croquet, volleyball, soccer, tennis, or baseball are useful for homeschooling families to have. Skates, jump ropes, balls, sidewalk chalk for hopscotch also provide children with exercise while they're having fun

Tools   Learning how to use a hammer, screw driver, saw, wrench, etc. is necessary for functioning in the adult world. If you have these sorts of tools, it can be very satisfying for your child to work with wood and make things. Of course, until they become skilled at using these tools, you will need to provide supervision and instruction. Access to garden tools and a space to have a garden might also be appealing to some children. Learning how to use kitchen tools is also an important skill. Again, with supervision, children can learn to use blenders, mixers, ovens, etc. to create yummy things to eat. A sewing machine is another tool that a child can learn to use. Holly liked to sew clothes for her dolls. When she was 8-9 years old, she learned to use the sewing machine and created pants and shirts for her dolls. My boys also learned to use the sewing machine at that age.

I started this chapter with a reference to Tom and Captain Najork and messing around. Messing around is what my children spent a lot of time doing when they were young. Their learning was the organic kind - from their experience with input from their dad and me. Through play, they absorbed all kinds of information and drew all kinds of conclusions. They had lots of time to play, including time to get bored. Homeschooling as we did it meant very little formal instruction.

Through their play, Josh and Noah learned all kinds of things about how paper airplanes flew. They had bags and bags full of them when they were about 8 and 6 years old. We provided information with books about paper airplanes, answered questions when asked, and watched as they flew their airplanes around the yard. They observed how the wind, the humidity of the air, the shape of the wings, and the kind of paper they used affected the flight of their planes. This was all self-generated and maintained. It led them to keep mental statistics about which plane flew the farthest under what conditions. They had fun making different styles of planes with different paper. Through this playful activity, they repeatedly demonstrated their ability to focus, their ability to draw conclusions from their observations, and their ability to make relevant comparisons. Things that children in school are asked to do, but in the context of teacher directed activity rather than self-generated activity.

It is through play that a homeschooled child has the opportunity to explore what interests him, and to do it with fewer arbitrary interruptions. Coaches and teachers who worked with my children often commented on their ability to concentrate and focus on the activity at hand. Because they had the freedom to follow their interests generated through their play, a book we'd read together, or a conversation, they revelled in the effort it took to learn a specific skill that interested them.

Let me give you some examples: Robin started percussion lessons when he was 12 years old. In the first six months after starting the drums, his practice time grew longer and longer until he was practicing 2½ to 3 hours a day. He organized his day to ensure that he had this much time to practice. He made a commitment to practicing because he enjoyed it. It was playing - playing the drums. Because he practiced so much, he progressed rapidly and also rapidly increased the volume of the material he was playing.

When Robin played baseball, he also gave it his full attention. He played beyond the regular Little League season when he was chosen to play on a 10 year old tournament team. He found it surprising that some of the boys seemed to be unable to concentrate - instead they would throw their gloves up in the air or do other things that showed that they were not paying attention to the game when they were out in the field. Baseball is a slow game. It requires a level of attentiveness that stretches the attention span of many children.

Holly took some rhythmic gymnastics classes for a while. She enjoyed it for about four months and then decided that she didn't want to do it anymore. One of the things she commented on as she was trying to decide if she wanted to continue was that it seemed as if some of the girls didn't really want to be there. They wouldn't follow instructions or they would do just the bare minimum of what was asked. Holly wondered why they kept coming. A good question!

When Josh and Noah were 6 and 4 they took gymnastic lessons. They listened and followed instructions. They wanted to learn how to do gymnastics. They loved the classes and the instructor became a very special person in our lives. She commented frequently on Josh's and Noah's attentiveness. She found it easy to teach them because they paid attention. They never expected to do anything but pay attention because they wanted to learn gymnastics.

My children's ability to be attentive comes from having the freedom to choose their activities, and follow their interests. My two sons who are musicians determined when they practiced and how long they practiced from the beginning. Their practice is their play. It brings them great pleasure. It is a continuation of what they did when they were younger, just a different form of play.

Ensure that there is playtime each day. People have often asked me just how I can managed to teach four children. I explain that most of the time my children played. Like a good nursery school teacher, I facilitated play by ensuring that our house was a safe place to play, there were things and/or others to play with, and then I stood back and let my children play. In between play times, I read stories, had discussions, or helped someone learn to read, write, sew, cook, or do math, etc. but by and large my children played.

This may be hard to visualize - after all most of us went to school for 12 years and spent hours learning and memorizing facts, information, and ideas. How could children possibly be ready to face the adult world if they play so much of the time? It's a difficult concept to digest..

Recognizing the importance of play, encouraging children to play by creating an environment in which play can take place means trusting that children are inherently good and want to become competent in the world. It means trusting the natural progression of their abilities and their desire for more understanding and knowledge.

I think about Gerald Durrell, the founder of the Jersey Preservation Trust renamed since his death to the Durrel Wildlife Conservation Trust (www.durrellwildlife.org). He wrote a number of books about his childhood years on the island of Corfu where he lived with his family in the 1930's. He was 10 when they moved there, 16 when they left. He explored the flora and fauna of the island to his heart's content. Although he had tutors at various times throughout those years, he was allowed the freedom to pursue his interest in natural history. He observed the lives of the animals and people around him, and had many opportunities to engage in conversations with people of all ages. From the stories he tells in his books, he had very few contacts with children his own age. Instead he had time, lots of it, to play. For him play was collecting and observing the wide variety of wildlife on the island of Corfu and feeding and taking care of his pets.

He once said in an interview that he wished he could give every child the gift of the childhood that he'd had on Corfu. He was fortunate, he discovered his passion, his calling in life, while he was young and he was allowed and supported as a child to pursue his interest.

Your children may not discover their passion or vocation early in life, but by giving them time to play you can support them to discover and then follow their interests. Who knows where that will lead?

Holly

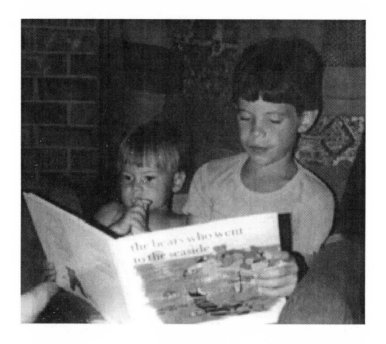

Robin and Josh

CHAPTER 3
Helping Your Child Learn to Read

Teaching a child to read is one of the major tasks of education. There are many methods to teach reading and there are many theories about how children learn to read. In this chapter, I will focus on

>•how you can help your child learn to read at home
>•how to motivate children to want to read
>•the signs of reading readiness
>•suggestions about how to work with your child to enable him/her to learn to read.

I hope that reading about my experiences with my children as they learned to read will help you. Please keep in mind that each child is unique - what works for one child may not work for another.

Before a child can learn to read, he needs to want to read. His experience with books and stories help determine his attitude toward learning to read. If his experience is positive, i.e., stories were read aloud to him at bed time or other times of the day and he saw the adults around him read, learning to read will be easier. It will be easier not because the act of learning to read will be easier, although it might be, but because the child has experienced that reading brings pleasure. It has built in rewards. This positive experience with the printed page helps to balance the work of learning to read and makes the effort worthwhile.

Reading is and has been one of my greatest pleasures. As a child I loved going to the library and coming home with new stories to read. I hoped that my children would come to enjoy reading. To that end - to help our children associate books with pleasure - my husband and I read aloud to them starting when they were very young (under a year old) and continuing into their teen years.

The books I read years ago about reading and how children learn to read seemed to say that given time, a child would just naturally begin to read if read to. Working under that hypothesis, I did a lot of reading aloud. When everyone was little, I read stories aloud at least 2-3 hours during the day as well as telling or reading stories at bed time. I read to my children every night until they were well into their teens.

Story time was a great way to soothe unhappy children. It gave us all quiet time together and a chance to recover our equilibrium. It was also a good way for me to spend time with older children as a younger one was sleeping or nursing. Even though they could easily read what I read aloud and had often heard it once, sometimes twice before, they still listened. It was time together we all enjoyed. Sometimes, I'd read for much longer than I intended because the story was exciting and I, too, wanted to know what was going to happen. There were many days when I read aloud anywhere from 4-6 hours per day broken up into smaller segments throughout the day. Since I love to read, this time was as wonderful for me as for my children.

Just as it's important for children to have positive experiences with books before learning to read on their own, reading aloud needs to continue beyond the time when a child can read on his own. Jim Trelease, author of *The Read Aloud Handbook*, writes about the importance of reading aloud to children of all ages. If you haven't already seen his book, you may find it helpful as he suggests many read aloud titles. I have listed some of our family's favorite read aloud books both within the text of this chapter, Chapter 6, in the bibliography, and in the appendix.

One of the reasons to continue to read aloud once a child has learned to read for himself is that the time spent together while you read aloud is a special time. It's important to make it clear to a child who is learning to read that he will not lose that special time with you when he masters reading, instead he will gain access to the world of books on his own. Reading aloud to children helps them to hear how language is phrased. It gives them a chance to hear words they may not be able to pronounce, and it allows them to listen to stories they may not yet be able to read on their own.

In order to learn to read, a child must be able to feel comfortable with language - to be able to predict what might come next, as well as learn how letters make sounds that make words. This is why reading aloud can be so helpful for children. They hear how words are used to tell a story. English is not an easy language to learn to read. There are so many exceptions to the rules of pronunciation. It's also a challenge to learn to read because the symbols that represent the sounds of language (letters) seem to have no rhyme or reason to the way they are shaped.

I found that as my children grew older, they did not, as some children I had read about, teach themselves to read by age 6. When Josh was 7½ years old, I began to feel uncomfortable that he was not reading on his own. I started to help him learn to read. We worked on phonics about 10 minutes a day. He was my first child, so I learned as much from the experience as he did.

At the start, I asked him to read one word on a page. He enjoyed the early reading books that rhymed such as the Berenstain Bear books about Papa Bear's errors and the book *More Spaghetti, I Say!* by Rita Gelman. He could easily predict what the word would be at the end of a phrase in these rhyming books and enjoyed reading that word aloud.

We moved on to more words as Josh was willing, ready, and able. Throughout this whole learning process, I wanted the way in which he was learning to read to be pleasurable. I did not want learning to read to be boring, a chore, or a matter for anger or argument between us. I kept looking to Josh's responses and reminding myself of my goal - that he learn to read with pleasure. I would remind myself that learning needs to take place in a pleasant atmosphere. I would remind myself that it was not a life threatening situation that he was not reading at 7 ½ -8 years old. Reminding myself of this and keeping my patience took a great deal of effort and discipline on my part. Just as I was asking my child to learn a new skill - reading, I was learning a new skill - helping my child learn to read.

When Josh was 8½ years old, he started reading *Charlotte's Web* by E.B. White. He jumped from easy-to-read books to books with many chapters because all of a sudden, it all clicked and he understood. He could read! He wasn't just carefully putting the letters together to form one word at a time, he saw whole words and could read sentences. This "clicking" with reading is what seems to happen when children master reading. For some children, it never comes. Although they can piece together words, they are not literate, they do not find pleasure in the printed word; the words do not flow off the page and into their minds.

I would love to know just how a child all of a sudden understands how reading works. I think of it as an "Aha" experience a sudden leap in understanding. I would love to be able to see just how this shift takes place. I have asked, but none of my children could remember even shortly after learning how, what happened to make it possible to read. Shortly after this happened for Robin he told me that "Just all of a sudden I saw how it all worked and I could read just about anything. Now there is no way I can see a group of letters and not read what it says, as long as it's in English."

I hoped that Noah, Robin, and Holly would learn to read on their own, but when they turned 7½ - 8 years old and hadn't started to read, I helped them start the process of learning to read. Robin, like Josh, began reading fluently by the time he was 8½ years old, reading way beyond his grade level. Noah read fluently by the time he was 12 years old. Holly made the transition from struggling to sound out the words to reading fluently when she was almost 11 years old.

It was worrying and uncomfortable for me when Noah was struggling to read. He so obviously found it frustrating and nerve wracking that I stopped asking him to read aloud to me after we tried it for a period of three to four months when he was 8 years old. He would read aloud a page or two of very simple beginning reading books, but he was so often unsure and hesitant. I reminded myself time and again of my philosophy of homeschooling - that children will learn when they are ready. I had to learn restraint and patience, and accept that Noah would learn at his own pace. He listened to many stories. His vocabulary was above what was expected for his age. His comprehension, his thought processes, and verbal communication skills showed that while he wasn't ready to learn to read, he was not a "slow learner." He just wasn't ready to read.

At 8½ years old, Noah began to change the size of the figures in his drawings after a few art lessons from a friend of mine. Noah had always drawn small detailed pictures. At 8½, he began to draw bigger pictures. He began to paint portraits from photos of Rembrandt's work as well as portraits from life at age 9½ - 10. His gift for art was evident in all he drew or painted from that age on. At 8, 9, 10, and 11 years old, he was not ready to limit himself to seeing things only from left to right and from top to bottom as one must when one reads. He needed time to let his artistic talent develop - time to be free of the pressure to limit his vision the way reading can limit it. I've read that elementary school teachers have noticed that children's art work often takes a turn for the worse after they start to read. It becomes more stilted and limited.

There are many children who struggle to learn to read at age 8, 9, 10, 11, and 12 years old. Not all of them are artistically gifted. It may be that for those children who struggle with learning to read that there are reasons for their difficulty with the printed page that we haven't yet discovered.

I don't think we know enough about how learning to read changes a child's perception of the world. I don't think we know enough about what learning to read does to a child's capacity for oral memory. People who live in a culture with an oral tradition have a capacity for memory and observation that seems almost supernatural to those of us in the printed world. I think we need to give children who struggle with the printed word time to develop at their own pace. Rudolph Steiner, a German philosopher who wrote about education as well as many other things, labeled learning to read as becoming linear. In the Waldorf schools which are based on his educational philosophy, children are not expected to learn to read (to become linear) before they are 9 years old or older.

I once read about some white men in the Arctic having trouble with a snowmobile. Even though the men who were riding the snowmobile had the diagram that explained the wiring and workings of the engine system, they could not figure out what was wrong.

An Inuit man asked them what the problem was. He took

hold of the plan upside down, looked at the engine compartment and instantly discovered what was wrong, fixed it, and the snow-mobile was working again. In the Arctic there are no fixed places for locating things, one needs to have an almost aerial perspective to be able to locate oneself in space. The Inuit man saw immedi-ately where the diagram and the actual engine didn't match. He saw the engine compartment in a different way than the men who were having trouble with the snowmobile. This story gave me com-fort when Noah didn't seem to be making any progress in learning to read. I drew comfort from this story because Noah was so adept at reading diagrams such as Lego instructions as well as so adept at art. He was obviously capable - he just wasn't ready to limit him-self to being linear.

We may be doing children a disservice when we ask them to read when they are not developmentally ready to do so. We may be making it very difficult for children to develop their own indi-vidual ways of perceiving the world. Yes, I know that being literate is necessary in our culture, and that being able to read is vital for adult survival in our world. At the same time, I don't think we need to be in such a rush to push a child who is obviously struggling. I think that if we give a child time, a child who is raised in a literate environment will more than likely learn to read. We need to trust that our children have an inherent desire to become competent in the world. If a child is struggling to master the skills of reading or refuses to even try, it often backfires when we push.

Children struggle with learning to read for a reason. Pa-tience is vital when you are helping your child learn to read as is a belief in a child's inherent desire to become competent. Many chil-dren are forced to learn to read before they are ready and they associate reading with drudgery, struggle, and humiliation. These children grow up to become adults who don't read. There are many adults who can read but do not choose to read even one book a year.

One of the reasons I chose to homeschool was to ensure that my children's self-esteem was not destroyed by agendas set for my children by others. So often children who are struggling with learning to read struggle because they are being asked to work within someone else's time frame. The reasons a child is not ready to read can be varied. It may be that a child has a need to develop his artistic vision, as Noah did. It may be that a child needs to develop other sorts of skills before turning to the task of reading.

The printed word doesn't give a reader the cues of the spoken word - voice tones, body language and breathing patterns. Some children may rely on the nuances that these clues provide more than others, making it hard to understand the printed word.

Some children do not think in words, they may think in flashes of insight, in feelings, in visual perceptions, in colors, in music, etc. Before a child is ready to start reading, he needs to be able to think in words. A child may be experiencing the world in a certain way and then translating that experience into words. To add learning to read to the process of learning how to think in words may be an overload to the system.

I think this is what went on for Noah. He was able to communicate quite well, but I don't think his primary internal language - his thinking process - was in words, it was in pictures or some sort of visual language.

Children may also need to sort out how they hear words. They may hear words much differently than how the people speaking to them think they are pronouncing words. Let me give you two examples of this. When Josh was working with beginning reading books we came across the word "just." He was quite surprised at the way it was spelled as he had always assumed the word was "dust." He was sure that whenever I used the word, I said it as "dust" as in "Dust a minute." We had a long drawn out discussion about this. It upset Josh to have to change his perception of this word. I am thankful that I could be gracious and supportive while he struggled to accept that what he had interpreted all these years as "dust" was actually pronounced as "just."

A friend of mine was asked to read something that her son, who was 10 years old at the time, had written - "Chrick or Chreet." It was Halloween, so she figured he must be writing "Trick or Treat." "Yes," he replied, "that's what I've written." He told her that that's how he heard it and he pronounced it for her as he had written it and said that that's how she pronounced it, too. It would be easy to get into an argument with a child and tell him that "Of course I don't pronounce the words that way. You are just hearing it that way and you are wrong," but it wouldn't serve any purpose. Denying the validity of a child's perception is pervasive in our culture, it damages many children.

If you discover that your child has interpreted a sound differently than you thought you pronounced it - be gracious and empathize with that child. It is confusing enough for a child to learn that his interpretation is not correct. He needs support not negative comments about his abilities.

You can help your child master the skills of reading by building on his or her inherent talents and strengths, and take into account any weaknesses. This is when you draw on the observations you have made of how your child learns. Homeschooling gives you the advantage of being able to work one on one with your child. You can tailor how you help your child learn to read to suit the child. That's why I stopped asking Noah to read aloud to me. He just wasn't ready to read on his own. Both my husband and I continued to read aloud to him.

When Noah was ready to read, he began to read with ease, not aloud, but to himself. At that time he was able to incorporate a linear focus without strain. I hope that reading about Noah's experience with learning to read will help you as you help your child learn to read. I hope it will encourage you to work with your child at a pace that feels comfortable to both of you and help you to accept that reading readiness does not happen at the same time for every child.

Reading readiness has many components.

- ability to think sequentially
- recognize and form the letters of the alphabet
- fairly stable understanding of the sounds associated with each letter of the alphabet
- able to think in words
- begin to notice printed words in environment

My children acquired some of these characteristics at an early age, years before they started to read. They knew how to write their names and the names of everyone else in our family by the time they were 3 or 4 years old. They could form the letters of the alphabet but didn't necessarily know the names of the letters. I named the letters by the sounds they made rather than calling a letter by it's name. A woodblock alphabet, *A Farmer's Alphabet* by Mary Azarian, was the source of the words I used to illustrate the sounds. (She designed this for her grade 1 classroom in rural Vermont.) "T (using the sound the letter made rather than the name of the letter) as in toad, etc."

When I started helping Josh, Noah and Robin learn to read, we used the beginning reading books that rhymed. I would point out how the word looked as they read the word at the end of a phrase. They could tell what the word would be because it rhymed and was easy to guess within the context of the story. We then moved on to working with homemade books of goofy stories based on simple phonetic words. "The cat sat on the fat rat on the mat." After a few months, Josh and Robin knew which sounds the various letters of the alphabet made. For Noah and Holly it was too confusing. From their point of view the letters p, d, q, or b were the same letter viewed from different orientations. They couldn't limit their perception at age 8½ to seeing these letters as being different. This coupled with the confusing phonetic rules of the English language was too much. However, Josh and Robin were willing to put up with the lack of logic and worked through our many beginning reading books when they were 8-8½ years old.

When I think back, I can still hear Josh read aloud a story about a little goblin from *Little Bear's Visit* by Elsie Minarik and Rita Gelman's *More Spaghetti, I Say!* Both of these stories have a sense of humor that appealed to Josh. I can hear Josh's dramatic expression and see his big brown eyes as he read these stories with ease, delighting all of us with his new found skill. As I mentioned before, within six months Josh was able to read *Charlotte's Web* to himself, one of his favorite stories at that time. He then read whatever he found interesting. If it was beyond his comprehension, he didn't finish it. If it was not to his liking, he didn't finish it. I never checked to see that he understood what he read nor did I censor what he read. He read so much when he turned 9 that Noah was quite often frustrated because Josh wouldn't play with him. He preferred to read.

Robin especially enjoyed the early reader *Hand, Hand, Fingers, Thumb* by Al Perkins. The repeating rhymes and rhythm "Hand Hand Fingers Thumb - One thumb One thumb Drumming on a drum - One hand Two hands Drumming on a drum. Dum ditty

Dum ditty Dum dum dum," made it easy to memorize. Robin (and later Holly, too) read the book aloud to me many times. (I had forgotten how much Robin loved this book until I started writing this chapter. I began to laugh because Robin was practicing on his drumset as I wrote.)

Both my husband and I read many of the easy-to-read books to our children when they were quite young. That meant that when they were ready to start reading on their own, they could chose a familiar story. We have especially enjoyed all the Little Bear books by Else H. Minarik; the books about Oliver and Amanda Pig by Jean van Leeuwen; the books about Frog and Toad by Arnold Lobel; the books about the Berenstain Bears that rhyme by Jan and Stan Berenstain; and the Nate the Great books by Marjorie Weinman Sharmat.

Your librarian can help you find easy to read books. Then you and your child can find books that you enjoy. As well as using the library, it's important to have books of your own. We found many beginning reading books for sale at garage sales and in thrift shops.

Part of learning to read is being able to anticipate what the author might say next, being able to think like the author. I was able to formulate this more clearly when I started writing this book on a word processing machine. I had to think in the ways that the machine was programmed. I had to move the machine's cursor in ways that didn't make sense to me. I wanted it to move differently in ways that seemed much more logical and direct to me, but I couldn't change the program. I learned to fit my thinking into the boundaries of the program.

When a child is learning to read, not only is that child learning to recognize the shape of the letters and the sounds those letters make, the new reader also has to think like the author of the book. Finding material that fit each of my children's thought patterns or ways of using language was a challenge.

Holly enjoyed working on her reading using the Little Bear books. The stories suited her way of operating in the world, the way she viewed things. Josh much preferred the Berenstain Bear rhyming books. The humor and rhythm of the verse appealed to him and suited his way of communicating.

That's why we had many kinds of early reading material in our house. Some author's thought patterns "fit" more easily with some children's thought patterns. To have to think in a way foreign to natural thought patterns as well as struggle to remember which letter makes which sound can make learning to read harder than it needs to be.

When I first began helping Josh learn to read I wasn't aware of this. I tried to find material that he enjoyed reading. As my other children learned to read, I began to observe how differently each of them think. These differences give diversity to our family life, enriching us.

Bio-diversity is recognized to be important for our survival on this planet. We recognize that we lose something precious when some of the myriad forms of life that inhabit the Earth become extinct. I wonder if we need to think about the diversity of human perception, intelligence, creativity, and thinking as well. Are we eliminating human diversity when we force children to read before they have established their own unique ways of thinking and perceiving?

Holly and I started working formally on her reading one morning while we were at Josh's harp lesson. I had brought with me photocopied pages of an illustrated alphabet from *Why Johnny Can't Read* by Rudolph Fleschman. I asked Holly to look at the pictures next to the letters. (I covered up the picture of the gun for the letter "G" with a goat.) I explained how the picture related to the letter sound, e.g., egg for the short "e" sound. I then asked her to draw me a secret one word message using the pictures to sound out the word. I thought the idea of a secret message might appeal to her. She had wanted to learn to read about a year before and was overwhelmed by all that was involved in recognizing the sounds the various letters made. She was hesitant to try anything else for a long time. She liked writing one word notes to herself or her dolls with invented spelling. I hoped writing a secret message to me using pictures would give her a way to move beyond her hesitation. It did. I closed my ears and eyes while she consulted with Robin.

After decoding her message, I made up a message for her using the pictures for the sounds of the letters. We continued making up secret messages for the rest of Josh's lesson time, laughing and having a good time. We continued this message writing over the next few days until Holly could consistently match the sound to a letter. We then went on to use the lists of simple three letter words provided in the back of *Why Johnny Can't Read.* Holly enjoyed the challenge of reading these words. The ones she mastered, I wrote on individual 3" x 5" cards and put in her "Word Box" (a file box, a suggestion from *Games For Reading* by Peggy Kaye. This book has many suggestions for fresh approaches to reading games written by a teacher who works with children who have been labeled as slow learners or unable to read.)

From this beginning, Holly began to read basic early readers. One of her favorites was *Sounds I Remember* edited by Bill Martin, Jr. This first book of the Sounds Readers, now out of print, had a lot of familiar nursery rhymes, songs, and pictures for storytelling. Bill Martin, Jr. suggested that early readers should group words in chunks of meaning. This gives visual clues to beginning readers to help them know which words belong together to make sense of the unfolding story.

Holly also loved *A Kiss For Little Bear* by Else H. Minarik. She read aloud to me about 10 minutes every day, sometimes longer depending on her interest. I helped her pronounce words when she got stuck. She was willing to have me correct her. Josh and Noah did not like to be corrected or helped, which meant that I had to learn to be very quiet and only offer suggestions when asked. It was very hard for me to learn to do this.

Holly read to me for 10 minutes a day for about four to five months, then stopped wanting to read aloud to me. About 6-8 months later when she was about 10 years old, she began to read on her own. She rushed into the room where I was to tell me that she had read 1½ pages in her book *"B" Is For Betsy* by Carolyn Haywood all by herself. She was very excited and pleased with herself. She then began to notice and read the signs when we went to the store or when we drove down the street. She began to think that she could make sense out of the words that she saw and so she noticed them. She began to spontaneously read words aloud. At age 10½, she read *Little House In The Big Woods* by Laura Ingalls Wilder to herself. She, like Noah, needed more time to switch to a linear way of thinking.

One of the things that was important for each of my children as we worked together on reading was that they retain ownership of the process of learning to read. I needed to observe and respond to their signals that told me that they had had enough. This required awareness on my part. I found it a constant challenge to know when to suggest that we continue and when to let go and stop because a child could not do anymore. I looked for signs of exhaustion, boredom, anger, or frustration and worked hard to ensure we stopped before these set in. I sometimes asked them to read just a little bit more when it seemed to me that things were going well and they were enjoying it. If they were willing, we would go on, sometimes for a very long time. If they were not willing, then we stopped. I would ask this after our 10 minute working period defined by setting a kitchen timer.

I didn't use this 10 minute working period everyday. We would do it daily for a week, then skip a few days and then start again. Then we would stop again for as much as a week or two and then start again. When both Holly and Noah clearly didn't want to do even 10 minutes of reading aloud each day, we stopped.

I could accommodate my children's individual needs and tastes as they learned to read. As we worked together, I had the opportunity to observe them closely, to learn about how they learned, and to listen to what interested them. We continued to build our relationship. When I asked them to do reading work that tore down our relationship, I realized that I was on the wrong track. Learning to read, unlike doing chores, was not necessary for the well-being of our family. Learning to read was for their individual benefit. They had a choice about learning to read. "I just love reading," Holly said as I drove her to a choir practice when she'd just turned 11. "Hurray!" I thought.

CHAPTER 4
Inviting Children to Write

Writing is a way to communicate. Something we sometimes forget when children first start to write.

Stories are the essence of communicating. Everyone tells a story. Lawyers must present their client's case in a believable fashion - tell a good story based on facts. How well the lawyer tells the client's story - clearly, succinctly, and sympathetically - is a big part of the outcome of a trial. A customer complaining about a bad product has to tell a story about why this product did not meet expectations. A grandmother wanting to share her perspective on life with a teenaged grandchild needs to find a way to tell her story so that it can be heard.

One of the best ways to begin the process of writing with children is to invite them to tell you stories. Children love to tell stories especially if they are encouraged. They want to share their perceptions of the world. Be a scribe and write down these stories as they tell them. This can start at any age. Very young children enjoy telling stories. Their stories may consist of just one word, but that doesn't mean the stories are less valuable than stories with more words.

Repeated experiences of having their stories recorded help children learn that we, the adults in their life, listen and value their words, their thoughts, and their stories. And it gives them the idea that writing down words allows others to hear their stories at another time.

Being a scribe for a young child can help you to preserve their thoughts. It also helps you gain insight into this child and gain a new appreciation for him or her. Being a scribe for a child is a way to build a positive relationship with a child. It gives children a wonderful feeling of importance to have someone recording their words. Be sure to write the date and the name of the author on the story before you start.

What to do as a scribe:
   Write down each word as the child relates the story.
   Do not change or edit the story.
   Do not criticize the action in the story.
   If you are uncertain what the child is saying, ask him to say it again.
   When the child is finished, read the story back to her.
   Examples of children's stories

And then story

Here's an example of an *and then* story by a three year old child.
   And then Miss Witch was going off in the woods
   and she heard an animal. And then she didn't know
   what the animal was. And then they found a nice
   stick to make into a Christmas tree. Then they found
   a Christmas tree in the woods and then they did
   chop it down. And then they went home and deco-

rated the Christmas tree. And then they went to bed. And the next day was Christmas. And then they got out and they had some balloons and sleds and some wires. And Santa Claus gave them another ax for Lulu because the other axes were all worn out and some skis and a telephone. And Santa Claus gave them two axes because the others were all worn out. And that was all the presents.

This is a typical *And then...* story. Children will tell this kind of story until they are 6-10 years old. This sequential narrative is a sign that a child understands that things progress from one thing to another. This understanding is necessary for a child to be able to learn to read. Pre-reading workbooks often include activities of sorting pictures to put in the correct order to tell the story. When your child is telling you an *And Then Story* she is using her ability to order and make logical sequences. Writing down these stories can provide a fascinating record of your child's progression in logical thinking as well as a record of their imagination

You can use this format to help stimulate a child's story telling:

This morning, I got up and got out of bed. And then I went to the bathroom. And then I washed my face.

If it is difficult for a child to tell a sequential story, then learning to read will be difficult because a child has not yet developed the sense that one thing happens after another thing. Children develop this ability at different rates.

Sometimes, as children get older, they like to play with sequential order and put things in that don't follow sequentially just to add some interest and fun to their story.   Children often add things that are totally unexpected without any direction from you. If your child is hesitant to do this, you could start the story, add an unexpected event and ask you child to go on from there.

This morning, I got up and got out of bed. And then I went to the bathroom. And then I washed my face. And then I saw there was a door in the mirror above the sink. And then it started to open.

Stories give a child scope for the imagination, a way to play inside their minds, a way to create a world to their own liking.

In chapter 8 of her book *A Child's Work: The Importance of Fantasy Play* Vivian Gussin Paley describes the power that stories have for children and how she used the children's own stories to encourage dramatic play.   Stories also help children process the events that happen in their lives.

The story and poem that follows were written by one of my sons after a visit from his Oma (the Dutch word for Grandma).

US Air
Once upon a time, Oma got on a big airplane in Boston to come and visit. And she slept overnight lots of times. And it didn't seem lots of times. And then they missed her when she was in the airplane.

<u>Song</u>
URS Air
Oh we were there
Oma goes, too
And I miss her very much.

Airport, I would like to go
On US Air
And go visit Oma.

My son turned four during his Oma's visit. She came to celebrate both his and his brother's birthdays. The words in this song still speak poignantly to me. Children of four have had so little time to experience things. Their perceptions and expressions of their feelings offer us a fresh look at the world and are often filled with a profound wisdom and simplicity. Writing down their thoughts is a way to preserve their unique take on the world.

Stories are a way for a child to try out different roles and see what happens. It's very important when a child is telling you an imaginative story that you don't interrupt the flow of words to try to bring reality into the story process. Let the child explore with his or her mind and write down whatever is being said. In other words, encourage children to develop their imagination and don't censor.

I wrote down many of the stories my children told when they were young. I wish I had written down more. Some of these stories were turned into books. Their father loves books, so some of the stories were made into books to give him as presents. I helped make the books they gave their dad. As everyone got older, they no longer asked me to be their scribe. They both illustrated and wrote the story in the books they made on their own.

These books are treasures. I enjoy looking at them now and reading through them. Some of them were written and typed using invented spelling. Even the author now has a difficult time reading what was written, although I can often puzzle it out. As I read through these books of invented spelling, I remember each child at that age and how differently they each thought and wrote down (encoded) sounds.

Creating homemade books:

Small Plastic Photo Album (holds 4" x 6" photos) 10-15 pages Find paper the right size or cut card stock to fit the pages of the photo album so that they easily slip in. Children can then start to work to create their story on each individual page. Two of my children liked to draw the pictures first and then tell me the story. Two liked to tell me the story first and then draw the pictures. The advantage of the small photo album method is that it is easy to fix any mistakes on a particular page. Just replace the page that the child is not happy with by slipping in a new one. Each sleeve easily holds two pieces of paper back to back.

On the opposite page is an example of a story written by Robin when he was almost 8 years old using this method. I removed the cards from the photo album and scanned them in to reproduce here with permission. I hope that this example of what the self-generated writing of an 8 year-old can look like is helpful to you. Children progress in their spelling abilities over time and with exposure to the words they read in books and other printed material.

Sewn binding

Once all the pages are organized and drawn and the story written, you can sew the edges together on a sewing machine if it is not too thick. Legal size paper folded in half creates an easy to hold size book. The pages can then be sewn down the middle easily by hand or by sewing machine or you can also punch holes and sew the book together with just a few bits of ribbon, yarn, etc. We found that drawing the pictures and writing or typing the words on a separate piece of paper and then gluing it into place made it easier to fix mistakes.

Stapled Binding

Like a sewn binding, you can staple the edges or the middle to create a book. A colored piece of construction paper or card stock makes either a sewn or stapled book more sturdy.

IT WAS HALLOWEEN
AND A BOE ANDGBAL
THEM WOT MLOG

THEA CAAM THA HOM
THEE NOCT ON THD DOR
TRICER TREET HIBE
YOU SOO

THEA CAAM TO A HOME
BTHE POT HM WER
A BOOT

OHEA THEAR HOT ON HOM
HOG
HOG
HOG

A WICH SWEAT
DORN AND PIT THEM
UP

ANDORP SHED PLAD TO HER
HOM

Story by Robin 8 years old

PASE
TO TWO
CAT
TWO
CAT
EFFER

THE WICH WAS TYERT FROM
CASTIG SPELS SO SHEE
DSKDT TO SLYP
WEN SHEE   WAS
A SLYP
SEM FRESOPINTHE DOR
GAATHE CATS
AND RAN OFR

THE FRES HET HER WAT
THE WICH HET SDE
THEAA SBD IT SAWERS
MOO MEGE HOGS
PASE MOW
BRE FO RALL THEM WER
AND
THEM
OL
LIFT
HAPPY
FOR
EVER

Unique Book Shapes

Create a fun shape – such as a snowman, hat, shoe, sock, etc. to use as a template for a special shape book. Cut out two shapes from sturdy paper such as card stock or construction paper and fill the inside with regular paper. Staple together and you have a unique book that can be used as a journal, for stories, etc..

Nonfiction Writing

Much of adult writing is nonfiction writing:

Lists

Appointments

Reminders

Dates

Thank you notes and letters

Greetings for special occasions

Some children find it fascinating to help write grocery lists. Very young children will sometimes write a list of items they want to purchase. Their lists are written with a great deal of intent although they may look like scribbles to us. Some children really enjoy making lists of names, toys, birthdays, etc.

Holly, more than her brothers, learned to read and write at the same time. She generated more spontaneous writing as she was learning to read than her brothers did. She was more oriented to verbal expression. She used to write lists of her dolls' names, their ages, their birth dates and phone numbers. She wrote notes from one doll to another and she had a pen pal for a while.

Let me digress here just momentarily to address the differences between my sons and daughter. My boys were oriented to building things, keeping statistics, playing games, observing patterns, etc. My daughter, while she did these things, was more interested in relationships between people and playing family type games. This difference is very striking. I have wanted to believe at various times in my life that men and women are not different because frequently being a woman has meant being less.

A book that I found fascinating, *Brain Sex, The Real Difference Between Men and Women* by Anne Moir, Ph.D. and David Jessel, discusses the physiological differences between male and female brains. This information can be used to help us understand how to work with the differences that exist between men and women rather than blame each other for the differences or value one above the other. More recently *The Female Brain* by Louann Brizendine describes, from one clinician's point of view, some of the research on the differences between the female and male brain.

Working with your children at home, you will notice differences. Some of these differences are related to personality, others are related to gender. Becoming more informed about the different ways men and women process information and events helps you to be more effective when you are helping your children learn.

Getting back to writing, invite your children to participate in making lists for items needed from the grocery store. If a child is uncomfortable with forming words with letters, you could suggest they make a pictorial list – draw a loaf of bread or a carton of milk. You can write the word beside the picture. This can help a child begin to connect the two things together.

When you get to the grocery store, you can give your child part of the list and encourage him to find the items while you look for other items in the same aisle.

Keeping a diary is also something that children might enjoy. Give your child a special notebook. I'd suggest starting small – a notebook that's 4" x 6" or 3.5" x 5" is less daunting than a larger notebook. A special pen or pencil can also make writing in a journal attractive.

Once I introduced the concept of keeping a journal, I left
it in my children's hands to go on from there. Some of them maintained a journal on and off over a few years. Others found they
liked to write at first but then they moved on to other interests.

If you are going on a trip, you might consider getting note-
books for everyone in the family and setting aside a time each day
for everyone to write in their journal. Or you could have a family
journal where each person can write or contribute thoughts that
others write for him or her. This type of journal can then be turned
into a memory book with photos of your experiences on the trip.

You can also use large index cards (5" X 7") and ask your
children to create postcards by drawing a picture of something they
saw or did that day. Use the lined side to write something about the
picture. If this sounds interesting, you might enjoy reading the
book *Stringbean's Trip to The Shining Sea* by Vera B. and Jennifer Wil-
liams to your children to introduce the idea. It's a book based on
postcards written by a boy to his parents and grandparents about
the trip he is taking with his brother across the country to the Pa-
cific.. Sometimes a child is inspired by watching or helping someone else put together a memory book. If you have a child who is
fascinated by this, help them start a memory book of their own.
Remember to keep everything simple. It doesn't have to be elabo-
rate, filled with the latest bells and whistles of decorations, stickers,
etc. Some children find creating decorative memory book pages
very fascinating.

When you need to send cards for special occasions or other
reasons, birthdays, anniversaries, thank you notes, etc., encourage
your children to make their own cards. A picture drawn by a child
and a few words about the person celebrating the occasion is more
meaningful than a card bought at a store. An acrostic poem using
the name of the person the card is for is a great way to make the

card special. There are examples of acrostic poems further on this chapter.

One of the things that makes writing interesting is descriptions. Here is an example of some ideas that you might find helpful in stimulating descriptive writing.

Encourage children to become keen observers
Go outside and look around
Ask children to tell you what they see
Write down some of the words they use

Describe an activity
Sledding

Going fast was exciting.
The sound the sled made on the snow was sort of a whizzing sound.

Make the sentences more active by using active verbs.

We sped down the hill on our magic carpet
The sled sizzled as it went down the hill.

Keep in mind that not all children will be interested in doing this. Some children would rather be left alone to think things through. And sometimes the best time to talk about language, descriptions, or active verbs is not when you are helping a child write but at other times, e.g., when you're reading outloud.

Another descriptive writing exercise is to ask why a child did or didn't enjoy an activity.

Write 3 lines with at least three words on each line.

What did you like about making cookies?
1. Mixing is fun!
2. They taste good.
3. They smell good.

I asked the adults in a workshop I presented about helping children write to write a description of something that happened in the morning before attending the workshop, to use three sentences with at least three words each. When I asked if anyone was willing to share what they had written, no one volunteered. They felt vulnerable, that their writing wasn't good enough. It's important to give children the same kind of choice. Don't demand to see their writing, instead ask and offer to share your results of this writing exercise with them.

When I ran a writing group for 7-12 yr. old homeschooling children, they were eager to share their writing with each other and with me. When they were sharing their writing, I asked them to read it to us so we could focus on what they had said rather than on whether or not it was spelled correctly.

Another writing exercise many children seem to enjoy is writing a descriptive poem using the acrostic method. Choose a word and using each letter of the word as the start of each new line, write something about the activity or word.

Here are some examples. The first two are mine written for demonstration purposes for a writing workshop. The others are samples from my children's writing.

Cookies taste so good to me.
Only they disappear too fast.
Oatmeal cookies are my favorite
Kind.
I love to bake.
Each time it's easier and the cookies taste
So good!

Sledding and sledding down the hill
Long lines form and I wait my turn
Everyone has mittens on.
Down we go, really fast!
Down to the bottom until we fall off.
Icicles forming on the trees.
Never stopping until we have to go home.
Got a new sled for Christmas.

OWL and **MOUSE** by Noah, Age 10

Over the
Woods silently
Looking for mice

Mostly scampering
Often found in the woods
Usually up at night
Sometimes stopping, sniffing
Eating flowers and seeds.

CROW by Josh, Age 12

Crows calling, flapping around,
Riding on air, hopping on ground.
Only the raven matches his black.
With wings outspread, he flies.

Here is a formula for writing a descriptive poem that children often enjoy. This is about a pet but it could be about an activity, a place, etc.

Pet Poem by Robin, Age 8

State pet's name	**Thumper**
Pet's colour	**Gray, white, and black**
Describe pet's size	**Medium size**
Where pet lives	**He lives in a cage.**
What pet eats	**He eats bananas, grass, and dandelions.**
Describe the way pet looks	**The way he looks is nice and cute.**
Add a wish	**I hope I'll have him as long as I live.**

Many children find that writing a poem is not as daunting as writing a whole story. They often enjoy writing poems just for that very reason.

Ideas for Stimulating Story Telling and Story Writing

Story cubes - Make a pattern of 6 squares similar to this picture and cut it out. Before folding to make a cube, write in each square. Use one cube for the characters – elf, king, princess, dog, cat, etc.; one cube for the problem in a story - can't find way home, trapped, stuck on the roof, etc.; and one cube for various settings – desert, ocean, island, city block, forest, etc. in which the story takes place. Then fold 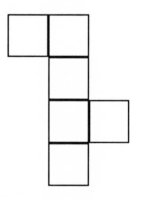 and tape each cube together and roll them like dice. You'll now have a character, a problem, and a setting.

You can also use the beginning of various stories to stimulate writing - storystarts. For example:

> Rufus had not learned to write his name in school, though that is one place for learning to write. He had not learned to write his name at home, though that is another place for learning to write. The place where he had learned to write his name was ... (from *Rufus M.* by Eleanor Estes)

> The village at the forest edge was quite a ways from the clearing. When the snow came ... (*Golden Bird* by Edith Brill)

> I came in and saw the parcel on the kitchen table. It was addressed to me! I ran over to ...

Let me emphasize again how important it is to keep reading to children after they have learned to read on their own. It's important for writing. You can read beyond a child's reading level, exposing him to new concepts, vocabulary and styles of language. Reading outloud helps children develop an ear for language and gives them examples of how our language works. Reading out loud provides:

> Vocabulary - *harum scarum gusts of wind*
> Pronunciation - *dough, through*
> Ideas - *Once upon a time there was a little river*
> Inspiration – *I must go down to the sea again*

A story has a beginning, middle, and an end. A story needs to have a character, a problem, and a resolution that takes place in a setting. These are story elements. You don't need to discuss these story elements with a child in any formal sort of way but it can be part of an informal discussion when you're reading together. Children absorb the structure of how stories work with exposure to stories that are read or told to them as well as by reading on their own. Professional writers say that the most important thing to do to improve writing is to read, read, read as well as write, write, write.

Writing also consists of mechanical and physical skills. To create writing readiness, give children lots of opportunities to work with pencils, pens, markers, etc. Drawing, painting, doodling, coloring are all great ways to learn how to hold these writing tools.

Encourage children to write their names and the names of members of their families. Remember that reversal of letters is common and that there is a wide age range in which children develop their interest and ability to write. For some, writing may never be their preferred method of communication. For most adults, writing is not something that is done frequently except in a work related setting.

Spelling comes over time. The more a child reads, the better his or her spelling becomes. An article by Stephen Krashen about spelling, *The Reading Spelling Connection,* sums up a century of spelling research (main points):

•Memorizing lists of spelling words isn't all that effective.

•Most people learn to spell by reading.

•Writers need to concentrate on writing and not worry about spelling until they are finished and in the revision stage.

•Ideas are more important than correct spelling

It's important to remember that while being a good speller is a good skill to have, it doesn't necessarily mean that you'll be a good writer. Over time, most people's writing skill improves the more they write. And keep in mind that English is a particularly confusing language to spell and pronounce.

Hints for Pronunciation for Foreigners
attributed to George Bernard Shaw

I take it you already know
Of tough and bough and cough and dough?
Others may stumble but not you,
On hiccough, thorough, lough, through?
Well done! And now you wish, perhaps,
To learn of less familiar traps?

Beware of heard, a dreadful word
That looks like beard and sounds like bird,
And dead: it's said like bed, not bead –
For goodness sakes don't call it "deed"!
Watch out for meat and grate and threat
(They rhyme with suite and straight and debt.)

A moth is not a moth in mother
Nor both in bother, broth in brother,
And here is not a match for there
Not dear and fear for bear and pear,

And then there's dose and rose and lose –
Just look them up – and goose and choose,

And cork and work and card and ward,
And font and front and word and sword,
And do and go and thwart and cart –
Come, come, I've hardly made a start!
A dreadful language? Man alive!
I'd mastered it when I was five!

My children learned the parts of speech through playing games of *Mad Lib*. These paper and pencil games consist of stories with blanks. Before reading the story, the players complete the list of words asked for, such as a singular noun, a verb, etc. It can be quite a funny and painless way to help your children begin to learn about the parts of speech. *Mad Libs* come with different themes and can be found in book and toy stores.

Helping your child learn how to use a keyboard efficiently is more than likely more beneficial than worrying about perfecting cursive hand writing. John Holt, in his book *Learning All The Time* published posthumously, suggests that printing is faster than cursive writing. (Cursive writing is based on copperplate writing done by scribes.) We did some time trials to see if his theory holds true. It was true for some members of our family and not for others.

I think it is important to realize that while you can help a child gain mastery of the physical skills of writing, knowing how to write doesn't mean that a child will choose to write. Helping a child learn to express himself is the other part of learning to write. Some children may find that words are not the form of choice for their expression. Instrumental music, art, movement, or song may suit them better than words.

Because I didn't want my children to feel that I was judging the validity of their work when they wrote things, I tried to remember not to correct their writing unless they asked. It was a struggle at first. I would never have considered changing a child's painting to make it look "right," why did I think I needed to change a child's writing? I would offer my help to correct spelling or add punctuation. Sometimes, I was taken up on my offer, often not.

Children in school are asked to do a lot of writing. I worried at different times about the fact that my children did very little writing. My boys showed very little interest in writing things down.

When Josh first started to learn to read and write, I asked him to write one sentence everyday (mechanics). He wrote "I hate this" rotating with "This is boring" for about a week. I stopped asking him to write. Instead, he began to read voraciously.

My children didn't choose to express themselves in writing very often when they were young. I frequently reminded myself that most adults do not express themselves in writing very often. It's usually done verbally or if written, in journal form that's not for public consumption.

Writing is THINKING then COMMUNICATING

Writing is more than putting words on paper. It's a final stage in the complex process of communicating that begins with "thinking." Some writers write everyday at a certain time no matter whether they have anything to say. Other writers spend a lot of time thinking before they begin to write and only write when they feel ready. There is no right way to write. However, most writers find that they need time and quiet to create a story. So if you are inviting children to write, give them time, quiet and a space to do their creating.

To create a book or story takes many hours. Some writers know the end of a story before they begin. Some writers start writing and the characters take the story in various directions. Some writers start one way and end up another. And some writers combine any number of methods. Writers often find they need to do some research to make their story more believable or realistic even if it they are creating a fantasy story.

One way to improve as a writer is to become a critical reader in the genre you want to write in. There are many online writing forums where you and your child can gain information about the writing process.

Nonfiction

I touched briefly on nonfiction writing when talking about creating a journal or memory book. Nonfiction writing is a broad field. Often nonfiction writing presents various points of view such as newspaper editorials that are told from a first person point of view or essays where one can speak one's mind about an issue. Instruction or identification manuals are examples of nonfiction writing. Research is usually involved when writing nonfiction. Even though the content is nonfiction, it's still important to tell a good story, so story writing helps both fiction and nonfiction writers.

Interviews are an example of nonfiction writing. Children can interview an older family member and then write a story based on that person's life. When doing an interview it is important to

1. Prepare ahead of time with a list of questions
2. Be a good listener
3. Be a good transcriber
4. Be able to develop the story

Family newsletters can be a way for children who are keen to write to share their writing. Help them put together a newsletter of stories, poems, interviews, opinions, descriptions, etc. and publish it to send to various family members. A newsletter is a great way for children to develop and learn

1. Writing skills
2. Keyboarding skills
3. Design skills
4. Editing skills

Remember that we want to invite children to share their thoughts. Accept that children make errors in their writing. Focus on what it is that's being expressed rather than the grammar. Ask a child if he or she would like you to do any editing. Treat the writing with respect and respond with genuine appreciation.

Model writing and let your child see you writing. Children learn what the people around them do. They want to participate in grown up activities so that they, too, can be grown-up.

In conclusion, writing consists of two parts: the mechanical side - letters, spelling, grammar, etc. - and the content. When you are helping your child learn to write, remember that it is the content, the message that's important. The mechanical side will come with time as long as a child is supported in his efforts. Give your child room to play around with words, writing styles, invented spelling and wait until asked to correct the mechanical side of the writing. Whenever possible be a scribe for your child so that he or she can see his or her stories written down. Help make the transition from verbal communication to written communication a gentle one, filled with encouragement.

T.T.T. by Piet Hein from *Grooks*

Put up in a place
Where it's easy to see
The cryptic admonishment
T. T. T.

When you feel how depressingly
Slowly you climb
It's well to remember that
Things Take Time

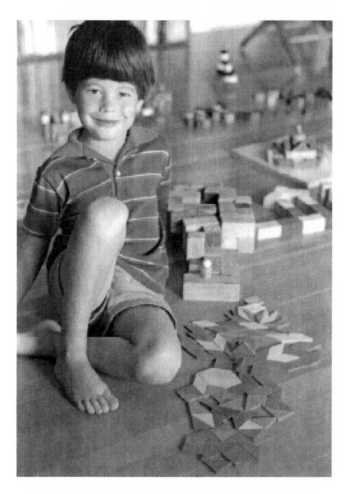

Josh

CHAPTER 5
Mathematics

When my children were toddlers, they enjoyed counting as we put cookies on a cookie sheet or as we cut a cake into pieces. They enjoyed having their fingers and toes counted or counting as we walked up and down the stairs. These activities and others like them are part of "math readiness."

Math readiness may not be something you thought about before. But, just as reading readiness is important, e.g., exposing children to stories, the printed page, words, etc., so is math readiness. In order for a child to understand about numbers and how they work, he or she needs to have had many experiences with numbers and number concepts.

Before you can help your child do the basics in mathematics -adding, subtracting, multiplying, and dividing - your child has to have an understanding of the one-to-one correspondence of numbers. Your child needs to know that 3 is 3 today, tomorrow, next week, and yesterday and that 3 is 3 whether the 3 objects are grouped close together or spread far apart.

John Holt in his book *How Children Fail* discusses the struggle that so many of the children he taught had with basic arithmetic. He described the panic that he saw in those children's faces when they would do arithmetic. They panicked because what happened during addition, subtraction, multiplication, or division seemed totally arbitrary, unpredictable, and confusing. They had no understanding of the one to one correspondence of numbers or the reliability of numbers.

Manipulative play with real objects is vital to developing an understanding of the predictability and reliability of numbers. Playing with things like Lego pieces, wooden blocks, beads, pennies, dolls, teddybears, pine cones, rocks, sticks, etc. gives a child first hand experience that the 3 rocks he had yesterday are still 3 rocks today. A child needs to have many experiences like this in order to understand what the number 3 represents.

This repetitive experience during play is a developmental step that parents can encourage by giving children time and space to play in, things to play with, and a vocabulary of words to use. It is a developmental step that cannot be short-circuited and taught – it must be learned and experienced by the child many times over.

Children who do not have an understanding of the one-to-one correspondence of numbers cannot add or subtract. They have no experience with the reliability of numbers and will often feel that there is a trick involved. If they could just learn the trick, then it would all be magically solved. The magic trick is to have a solid understanding of the one-to one correspondence of numbers.

With this solid understanding of the one to one correspondence of numbers (3 is 3 is 3 no matter how far apart or close together) and the reliability of numbers (3 is 3 is 3 whether it is today or tomorrow), addition, subtraction, multiplication, and division can be learned. A problem that is solved today (5+3=8) will have the same solution tomorrow. It is solid and predictable.

As well as manipulative play, it helps to give your child a vocabulary for arithmetic. Let me give you an example of how a simple conversation regarding cookies can help increase a child's understanding and mathematical vocabulary. Let us suppose that a 3 year old has 5 cookies. He eats 3 of the cookies and has 2 left.

Describing the situation mathematically, "You had 5 cookies, then you ate 3 and now you've only got 2 left." If there were more cookies and my child was hungry, I'd offer more saying, "Here are 2 more cookies to add to the 2 you have left. That makes 4." If this is casually done, then over time a child develops a vocabulary to use. He observes numbers and their properties while he plays. Now that doesn't mean a child will necessarily talk about these concepts, but he will incorporate the vocabulary and use it to describe what he observes as he plays. All of this takes place almost subconsciously and most of the time internally although toddlers who have heard numbers will begin to count - "1,2,4,8,3,10".

One of the ways to incorporate play with numbers into your daily life is to use finger plays like this one from *This Little Puffin* by Elizabeth Matterson.

> Here is the beehive. (hand closed in a fist)
> Where are the bees? (look at the fist)
> Hiding where nobody sees. (look around the fist)
> Here they come creeping out of their hive
> (slowly lift up each finger)
> One, Two, Three, Four, Five
> (extend each finger as you count)
> Bzzz (make your hand fly around)

Before starting any formal arithmetic work, I encourage you to observe your children to determine their understanding of numbers. Find out through observation if they have a solid grasp of the one to one correspondence of numbers. If your child is under the age of 5 or 6, begin to introduce the vocabulary of arithmetic, if you have not already done so. "Let's count how many apples we have left in the fruit bowl. Now let's subtract the 8 we need for a pie. Let's count how many we have left." Describing your activities like this may take practice if it is not part of your normal vocabulary, but it is worth the effort.

If your child is older, you can still introduce the vocabulary of arithmetic, but it may seem a little forced. Mathematics is a way of describing and defining the events that take place in our lives. Just as I gave my children the names for objects and their colors, I gave my children names for the process of addition, subtraction, multiplying or dividing. It wasn't a formal lesson, just a part of everyday life.

As well as vocabulary, I provided opportunities for us to play with mathematical concepts. One of the activities my children enjoyed was stacking up pennies to see how high the stack was for a nickel, dime, quarter or dollar. We spent many hours playing with coins when each child was between 3-6 years old. It was an activity they really enjoyed.

While we played, I made comparisons and encouraged them to tell me about the differences they noticed in the various stacks of coins they made. It was a very satisfying way to see how numbers worked and the relationship of pennies to nickels, dimes, and quarters. This was all done at a very slow and relaxed pace while we sat on the floor. By the time the boys were 6 years old, they could easily determine if they could afford to buy a toy that they wanted. They did this figuring in their heads.

When my sons worked on a number problem in their minds, they often thought in terms of pennies or coins. Holly found it easier to answer if I described a problem in terms of families of animals or teddybears. For example "There's a family of 5 cats - a mama, papa, and 3 sisters. Two of the sister cats go off into the bushes to explore. How many cats are left?" Just as when you help your child learn to read, you use material that fits his or her thought patterns, you look for ways to present number information in ways that appeal to your child. Cookies were a favorite way for everyone in our house to learn about adding, subtracting, multiplication, and division.

Games were another way we did math. One mental math game we enjoyed was to give each person who wanted to play a number question, for example "How much is 3+5?" as we rode in the car to the grocery store or sat around the kitchen table after supper. Each member of the family who wanted to play would ask someone else a number question in turn. The only rule was that the person asking the question had to know the answer to his or her own question. My husband and I tailored our questions so that each child could answer the question.

I always found it amazing to see how quickly even a younger child grasped some of the basics of arithmetic and wanted to participate. At age 4, each of our children could do simple division problems in his or her head. If we have 2 cookies and 4 children, how many cookies does each child get? As the children mastered addition and subtraction of numbers to 10, the questions in our game became more difficult. They no longer needed to refer to actual objects (like their fingers) to solve the problem, they had a mental grasp of what each number stood for.

This number game and other games such as card games as well as various discussions of numbers and how they worked were not "lessons," they were a part of our family's daily life. This way of studying mathematics may seem haphazard yet my children developed an understanding of numbers and how they fit together without much trouble and at a fairly early age. They learned these things as they played.

I didn't start doing written math with my children until they

were about 7½-8 years old. They were fascinated by the workbooks that they saw in our local K-Mart. They were eager to do the
exercises in workbooks like *The Golden Step Ahead Books*. They would
work intensely for a few days, finishing one and sometimes two
workbooks. Then their interest would wane.

Some of them enjoyed doing each problem in the workbooks, others did one or two, figured out what they were supposed
to do, weren't interested in doing more and then went on to the
next page. Months passed before they would show another flurry
of interest. These workbooks gave me an idea of what each child
knew how to do and provided an opportunity for me to help them
learn some of the skills they wanted to learn. Once they learned a
new skill and practised it enough that they understood the proce-
dure and could do it easily, they weren't interested in doing more
problems.

By the time I was 8 years old, I had memorized the multiplication tables up to 12. I was concerned that Josh did not have this
information memorized when he was 8. I had to reassess my assumption that one must learn these tables by age 8 or else. (I am
not sure what the "or else" was. I have never known just what the
"or else" is. I have always assumed it to mean that some sort of
catastrophe will befall one, but so far I haven't noticed that any of
these catastrophes have happened.) I came to the realization that
memorizing the multiplication tables did not mean understanding
multiplication. At age 8, Josh's grasp of how numbers worked and
the patterns they made was much more extensive than my own at
age 8. He eventually memorized the multiplication tables in the
process of playing the games programmed into a Snoopy Calculator that we had.

One of the things I used to help my children learn multiplication was to write out the times table on a piece of graph paper.
This can then be used as a reference. When Holly was 10, she

decided to make a times table like this. I was making peach jam and thinking and measuring and she was busily working at the kitchen table asking me questions. She worked along happily; I made jam happily. I thought about how often my children ask me to help them learn something while I am in the middle of doing something I can't stop.

Holly made some very astute observations about the pattern of the numbers as she filled in the squares. She asked me a few times if her multiplication was correct and I found myself answering yes, knowing it wasn't quite right but at the same time counting out spoonfuls of pectin and not being able to count and multiply at the same time. As soon as I didn't need to concentrate so hard on what I was doing, I'd ask her to ask me again what she had just asked me and we corrected my errors.

This example epitomizes much of our homeschooling. It rarely happened that I sat down and "taught" my child something. My children often asked a question and were ready to absorb the answer during the "in between" times or the times when I was thinking about something else or concentrating on something. This can either drive you quite crazy or it can make you laugh.

When the boys (at ages 11-12) were ready to learn long division, we worked together for about 15 minutes and then they had it figured out. They already understood multiplication. They had done lots of division problems in their heads. While learning to do division on paper was new, they were already familiar with division having done it mentally so often.

Learning the skills of how to solve arithmetic problems often requires lengthy explanations. One of the benefits of homeschooling is that you can take the time to answer a child's questions and ensure that he or she understands. Let me give you an example of what I mean.

My brother, who designs and builds both hardware and software for computers had a difficult time with his teacher when he was in grade 5. He kept getting the answer to subtraction problems wrong by one digit, e.g., 19-11=7. He tried to explain to his teacher that he needed to know where to start from when subtracting. Was he supposed to subtract between the numbers or include the numbers. He asked his teacher whether he was supposed to be counting the poles and the lines or just the lines in between the poles.

She didn't understand what he was trying to say and just told him that he needed to memorize the facts. She accused him of not studying because he kept getting the wrong answers. This teacher had no idea what my brother was asking. He didn't have the vocabulary to explain it when he was young. His teacher told him that he was being difficult. She didn't have the time to discover just what he was trying to ask her.

Perhaps you've had a similar question. We had them often - how many days it is until a birthday or Christmas or some other special event? Different people in the family gave different answers. Each answer is correct, but it's very confusing. It was important to define the question more clearly - *Do you want to know how many sleeps it is, or how many days between today and the special day, or how many days it is from today not including today until the special day, etc.?*

We also had discussions about what is being asked in a problem such as 19-11=? Are we counting how many are left after you take 11 from 19? Then it would be 8. Are we asking how many numbers there are between 19 and 11? Then it would be 7. Are we counting how many numbers between and including the numbers 19 and 11? Then the answer would be 9. I explained to my children that the problem 19-11= means how many are left after you take away 11. Using cookies as an example - you have 19 cookies and eat 11, how many are left?

I had not anticipated these mathematical discussions. I thought I would just show my children how to add, subtract, etc.

without any discussion. I never realized how interesting mathematics could be and that what had seemed to me to be a simple problem could be so complicated. These discussions were an introduction to logic and defining terms and helped me to carefully explain what was wanted when we did arithmetic problems together.

If you are uncertain about just how much your child would be expected to know about arithmetic at a given age if she were going to school, you could consult a math text book or work book appropriate for your child's age. However, keep in mind that like with reading, children mature at different rates in their ability to understand math. You can't force understanding. You can encourage it and support it's development by providing what I have already mentioned – time to play and things to play with as well as words, a vocabulary, to use to describe mathematical activities.

As well as math textbooks, you might find the series of books by Marilyn Burns *Math for Smarty Pants*, *The I Hate Mathematics! Book*, and *The Book of Think* helpful. My husband, Larry, uses some of the exercises in these books in his classroom.

I enjoyed three math textbooks for high school students by Harold Jacobs *Mathematics A Human Endeavor*, *Algebra*, and *Geometry* published by W.H. Freeman and Company, 660 Market Street, San Francisco, California 94104. I liked Jacob's approach. His textbooks are filled with cartoons, and he explains things clearly. The answers to many of the problems are listed in the back of the book which is helpful. The teacher's edition has interesting examples that expands the material presented in the student textbook. You can find his books for sale online through various homeschooling supply stores.

While I looked through these books and enjoyed them, none of my children showed a great deal of interest in his textbooks. When they were younger, their math tended to be related to roll playing games that used dice, logic puzzles, games, design, or how much money they had to buy a certain toy or game they wanted. With their basic understanding, they learned other higher level math skills as the need arose.   My daughter learned math through play with her brothers and by keeping track of her finances.

There are many math curriculum products and programs available. Before purchasing any of this material ask around to find out what other homeschoolers have found works for them. And look for secondhand curriculum. Many homeschooling families find that they spend money on prepackaged math curricula only to find that it is never used beyond the first month.

If you are uncertain of your ability to teach mathematics to your child, remember textbooks are designed to teach. You don't already need to know the material before starting. If you find that you and your child get stuck, reach out to others for help. It's OK to ask for help. It models for your children that when you don't understand something or need more information, you turn to other resources to find the answer or help needed. A great lifelong skill to acquire!

If you are uncertain, you may want to take a basic math refresher course. You might also consider that there is nothing as effective in helping you learn something than teaching it to someone else. You can start simply with basic addition with your child while you bake cookies or as you count pennies. You don't need to worry when your child is young how you will ever manage to teach her algebra. As you work with your child in a casual and relaxed way to explore the world of numbers, you may find that your confidence increases so that by the time your child is older and ready to tackle algebra you are, too.

If you find that rather than getting excited by exploring the world of mathematics, you want to run and hide because you are uncertain about your abilities, and wonder if you can still homeschool if you feel like this, you do have alternatives other than sending your child to school. You can find someone who is willing to tutor your child in this subject. Being a homeschooling mother doesn't mean you have to do everything yourself.

When Robin wanted to learn higher math, I asked Josh to help Robin learn the skills necessary to be able to do the problems on the Gauss Math Tests (University of Waterloo, ON Canada) from past years. Josh was more than happy to do this. Robin was willing to learn these skills from Josh. He was used to Josh helping him learn how to play various games. This was just another game.

Mathematics is not just numbers. Logic and deduction are part of it. The books about Encyclopedia Brown by Donald Sobol are great read aloud short problem stories that can be fun for children to think about and try to solve. These books are about a 10 year old detective and the problems he solves in his small hometown.

Martin Gardner, who wrote for Scientific American, wrote about recreational mathematics. His work may appeal to an older child, see the bibliography. Raymond Smullyan has written books about logic that an older child may find fascinating - *What is the name of this book?*.

As well as arithmetic, mathematics consists of spatial relationships. Puzzles, origami, making quilt squares, designing buildings, drawing, cutting out paper dolls, etc. all involve spatial relationships. As a child plays with puzzles or building blocks, he begins to develop an understanding of how things fit together, he develops a sense of the relationship of one thing with another. Compass constructions and mazes also involve an understanding of spatial relationships and can be fun for children. (See the bibliography for recommended books.)

Playing games was the most consistent form of mathematics we did. Board and card games can be an almost invisible way for a child to learn and understand numerical sequence, addition, and subtraction. Playing games develops the ability to think logically and sequentially, a necessary part of mathematics. As you and your child have fun, you help your child improve his or her math skills. I have listed a number of games that we enjoyed below. The board games I list may be available at thrift shops affording you an opportunity to try games with less financial risk.

I haven't listed any computer math games because by the time we had computers, my children were teens. The most sophisticated electronic math program we had when my children were little was a Snoopy calculator made by Texas instruments I mentioned earlier. It had some great programs for reinforcing and solidifying basic math facts.

My concern about computer games is that it isolates a child. Young children, especially, need to have interactions with real, live people and play games within the context of a relationship rather than sitting in front of a monitor. A computer also does not give a child real things to manipulate and count. It works in symbols and as numbers are also symbols for real objects, it can be a very confusing way for a child to acquire an understanding of how numbers work. There are no real objects to hold, feel, and move about.

The Atlantic Monthly July 97 issue had an article "The Computer Delusion" by Todd Oppenheimer that discusses computers at length and how they have not significantly improved teaching or learning. This article won the 1997 National Magazine Award for reporting in the public interest. Oppenheimer published a book in 2003 *The Flickering Mind -Saving Education from the False Promise of Technology* which looks interesting. One of its premises seems to be that children need real, hands-on manipulation of objects to learn and understand math.

An article posted on the website for lifelong learning at the University of Colorado http://l3d.cs.colorado.edu/philosophy.html#1.4, also has information about technology and learning and how it has not done much beyond repackaging old methods. I would urge you to spend money on math resources that are hands on - things like multi-faced dice, blocks, Lego - before spending money on math software. Check online reviews for various math software and check in with other homeschool families to find out what they have found helpful.

Besides helping my children with many basic mathematical skills, playing games also gave them experience in negotiating with others and an appreciation of the need for structure and rules. They discovered that without rules, arguments became the activity instead of the game we intended to play. Even when rules are established, there is room for interpretation as, for example, the call of balls and strikes in baseball by the umpire. Games can be a great forum for learning the art of consensus.

When all my children were little they enjoyed games like Red Light Green Light, Mother May I, and Kitty In The Corner. These were simple games with easy to understand rules where everyone had a chance to participate. As Josh and Noah grew older, we started to play more complicated games that required more skill - such as card games. These games were on the whole competitive. We did try various commercially produced cooperative games, but Josh and Noah found them very boring after the age of 5. Holly and Robin enjoyed cooperative games longer. When Holly and I played together, she often turned a competitive card game into a cooperative one.

I struggled with my conscience about teaching my children competitive games. I didn't like setting up someone to lose. I found it hard to help the loser deal with his emotions and would often suggest that we play something else. Josh and Noah wanted to keep playing competitive games and persisted in spite of the tears and frustrations. As they grew older they acquired more game playing skills and gradually learned to cope with their feelings about losing.

Robin began playing board and card games with his older brothers when he was about 4½ years old. He told me that he never expected to win when he was younger, he just enjoyed being included. As Robin grew older winning became more important so we set up handicaps for some games according to the player's age and skill level to compensate for varying age and skill levels. As his skill level increased, Robin no longer found handicaps necessary. It's something you may wish to consider doing in your family.

At the end of this chapter, I have listed a number of games we enjoyed playing. I hope you find some that your family will enjoy. Some people thrive on certain kinds of games that others find boring. Some thrive on competitive games, some don't. Try some of these games and observe your child to see which ones bring pleasure.

When choosing games from this list, please remember that the age range is an approximation. What will work for a 5-year-old who is third in a family may not work for a 5-year-old who is first and vice versa. Children who have watched older siblings play games already have a framework for how to play a game.

Learning the skills involved in playing games is something that takes time. Being able to wait one's turn, being able to count, being able to match colors are all skills that playing games rely on and strengthen. Part of the fun of being a homeschooling parent is that the time you spend playing games with your children is part of their education.

I hope that this chapter has given you an idea of where to start with mathematics and has given you enough information to feel comfortable about helping your child learn about mathematics. As you work with your child, remember to work from a place of patience and calm. If whatever you are doing isn't working and you and/or your child become frustrated, change activities. There's a book called *Always Change a Losing Game* which says it all in the title. Have fun! Enjoy the fascinating world of mathematics. It is a much bigger world than one limited to arithmetic.

Explore spatial relationships with puzzles, origami, sewing, building with blocks, decorating a cake, or other things. Play games like poker or gin rummy and learn about predictability and probability as you play. Once you start thinking about it, you will notice opportunities to see the world in a mathematical way. Seed pods in the garden become representatives of geometric shapes. Baking cookies becomes an exercise in times tables and addition, etc. Like a child who is starting to read and suddenly notices all the words everywhere he looks, you will see the many ways mathematics are a part of your life.

One of the great things about doing math informally by using games, doing puzzles, or observing nature is that you can show a child that it is OK to make mistakes (as in choosing the wrong puzzle piece and then finding it doesn't work). It has made mathematics so much more pleasurable and exciting for me. It tickled my fancy to know that when I did a puzzle with my children we were doing math. Mathematics is so much more than computation. It is way of perceiving and defining the world. And now for that list of games.

Games without props
Games that can be played almost anywhere

Animal, Vegetable, Mineral from age 3-4 up. This was a favorite guessing game in our family when the children were young and came with me to do errands. One person chooses an object and decides its category - animal, vegetable, mineral. The others ask a question with a 'yes' or 'no' answer, one question at a time in turn. Eventually the other players discover what the object is or the other players give up. A new player chooses an object and the game starts again.

For younger children, it may be easier to first start with just one category such as animals and define clearly just what will fit into the category of animal. This game lends itself to great discussions about what things are made of "In what category is a Lego block?" and can be a fun way to pass the time as you are driving around doing errands. Limit the numbers of players to keep everyone involved. A larger group means that everyone has to wait too long for a turn. We found 4-5 players were as much as we could manage.

Charades Ages 5 and up. One of my favorite games. We play in teams of two or three with each team choosing a book, song, or movie title to act out. The teams go to separate parts of the house to discuss how they will act out the title. When everyone is ready, we all go into the same room and start.

Each team presents the charade they have chosen. The other teams all try to guess what the title is. No score is kept. No points are won or lost. We just have a lot of fun and laughter. It's a great game for a mixed age group. Even young children can be included as part of a team and can act out the charade with the other team members. Having a mixed age team also has the advantage of helping a younger child learn how to act out words, what strategies to use when words rhyme or sound like other words, etc.

I Spy Ages 3 and up. "I spy with my little eye, something that is green." The other players ask questions with "Yes" or "No" answers until the object is found. I found it interesting to observe my children develop systematic approaches to locate the object in a room by asking questions that eliminated parts of the room as well as asking questions that eliminate certain categories of objects. This game and others like it that rely on answers to yes or no questions help children develop problem solving techniques.

These games were invaluable in developing some of the

basic skills required to do mathematical problems. The advantage of playing these sorts of games in a mixed age group is that older players can model problem solving skills for younger ones. We played these sorts of games for more hours than I can count. No wonder my children think of problem solving as an interesting challenge - a game.

Kitty In The Corner   Age 3 and up. We started playing this game after reading The Little House Books by Laura Ingalls Wilder. You need room to play this game. Find a space that has one less "corner" than player. (You don't have to have actual corners, you can designate certain places in the room as a corner.) One player is in the middle and the other players are all in their corners. The person in the middle shouts out "Kitty wants a corner." All the players have to move to a new corner. The person in the middle runs to a corner as well. The player left over goes to the center and begins the game anew by shouting "Kitty wants a corner." It's a great way to burn off energy during inclement weather. Make sure the place you are playing is safe for running. Because the game moves so fast, everyone gets a chance to both be in a corner and be in the middle fairly often.

Mother May I?   Ages 2 and up. I remember playing this game frequently with Noah and Josh when they were very young. They thought it was a great game. One player is the *mother*. *Mother* stands in a certain spot. (We played in a hallway with *mother* at one end.) The other players line up at a defined distance from *mother*. *Mother* then calls each player by name, in turn, and tells them that s/he can take a certain number of steps. "Noah, you may take 4 steps." This player must then ask "Mother may I?" *Mother* then replies with "Yes, you may." or "No, you may not. You may take 2 steps (or whatever number chosen)."

If the answer is 'yes,' the player moves the numbers of steps *mother* has said. If the answer is 'no,' the player again asks "Mother, may I?" in response to the number of steps *Mother* has said. If a player does not ask "Mother may I?" and begins to move the 4 steps suggested, he must go back to the beginning and start again. Eventually one player will reach *Mother*, tag her and that player now becomes *Mother* and the whole game starts over again.

This game can be varied by being creative with the kind of steps *Mother* asks the children to take - baby steps, giant steps, whirly twirly steps, hops, etc. It can be very powerful for a small child to be in charge and have everyone moving just the way he wants.

This game as well as Kitty in the Corner and Red Light Green Light can help a young child begin to understand the framework of how a game is played. It is a game that is physical and fairly simple. Adult participation (or that of an older child) ensures that the game does not lead to arguments about the sizes of the steps. My children enjoyed this game until they were about 8 years old. After that, it lost it's appeal.

I remember playing this game at school during lunch and recess through 6th grade. We played outside on a large paved area the size of a basketball court with about 15-20 girls.

Guess Who? Ages 4-5 and up. Another yes and no question game. This time one person chooses a character from a book and the other players try to guess who it is by asking yes or no questions. The only rule we established was that the character had to be from a book that was familiar to all the players.

Red Light Green Light Ages 4 and up. One person is *It* and stands in a particular spot. The other players line up at least 10 feet away. *It* turns around, away from the other players so that his/her back is to the other players and calls out "Green Light." The other players move toward *It* and try to tag *It*. *It* can say "Red Light" at anytime and turn around to face the other players. Any player seen moving by *It* is told to go back to the starting line. *It* then turns around again and says "Green Light." Make sure rules are established that specify that there is no pushing or shoving. An adult playing the game helps set the tone of having fun without anyone getting hurt.

Sardines Ages 2 and up. Sardines is a form of hide and seek where *It* hides. The other players find *It*, and then hide with *It* until everyone is hiding. The first person to find and hide with *It* becomes *It* for the next game. Fun to play both inside and outside. My children have enjoyed games of sardines and hide and seek since they were very small. Both of these games are good games to play with a mixed age group.

Board Games

Following is a list of some of the commercial board games our family has enjoyed. Some of these games may no longer be available new but can be found secondhand at garage sales or thrift shops. This list is only a beginning guide. I know there are lots more games out there for families to enjoy playing together.

Casino Yahtzee ages 7 and up. A game of chance using dice, up to 4 people can play at once.

Checkers, Chinese Checkers, Chess, Go ages 5 and up. We used handicaps for some of these games to balance the skill level between players.

Clue A player needs to be able to read or have a partner who can read in order to play. Can be played by up to 6 players. A game that can develop logical reasoning, deductive thinking.

Cranium ages 8 and up. We first played this game in 2006 with family friends. A great game to play with teams composed of mixed ages. Lots of fun!

Hey! That's My Fish ages 8 and up, up to 4 can play. Penguins try to control hexagonal pieces to have the most fish - short game

Max A cooperative game for ages 3-4 (with adult help) and up. It involves the players working together to get the little animals home before Max, the cat, catches them.

Scotland Yard ages 10 and up. Best played with only two players, otherwise it becomes a long and tedious game. Players use maps of the underground transit system and streets of London. One player is the detective, the other is the criminal.

Settlers of Catan ages 10 and up for 3 or 4 players. A good introduction to the many wonderful European board games.

Sleeping Grump A cooperative game for ages 4 and up with adult help. Players try to get the treasure before the giant wakes up.

Survive ages 5 and up. Up to 4 players. The players attempt to get off an island that is sinking before a volcano explodes. Could be played cooperatively. Out of print but worth looking for.

See boardgeek.com for more info on board games.

Card Games

Here are some of the card games that we've enjoyed that use a regular card deck. I have listed approximate ages. Libraries carry numerous books about how to play card games, so I won't duplicate that information here. Grandparents or other older people can be a good resource for new card games. A cardboard box can serve as an effective screen so that a small child who cannot hold his or her cards in his or her hands can spread the cards out and no one else can see them.

Crazy Eights from 5 up

Cribbage from 6 up, need to be able to add up to fifteen

Euchre from 7 up

Hearts from 6 up - always a difficult game for me to play as I don't like giving someone the Queen of Spades to make them lose.

Kings in the Corner from 5 up. Can be played cooperatively.

Pig from 5-6 up

Poker from 6-7 up

Solitaire from 7 up

Spit from 8 up

Card Games With Unique Decks.

Phase 10 from 7 up. This game kept Holly happy for hours when she was 7 years old and her brothers were all sick. Can be played cooperatively by not keeping score and turning the cards face up.

Old Maid from 4-5 up. Simple and fun as long as children can cope with losing.

Uno from 4-5 up. A commercial version of Crazy Eights. Because the numbers are so big and the colors so easy to identify, it might be a good way to start playing with cards. Robin liked this game a lot when he was about 4 years old. We took out the "pick up 2 or 4 cards" and played with our cards face up in front of us so that we could help each other.

Wizard from 9 and up. It's the "ultimate trump game" and fun for the whole family.

Noah Lego Bird
Math becomes art.

CHAPTER 6
The Arts
Music, Art, Dance, Drama, and Phys. Ed.

The arts provide an avenue for expression, a way for a child to create or express his or her response to life, a way to give meaning to life. Children naturally express themselves in creative ways. It's as natural to them as breathing. If we provide materials, space, lessons (when needed), and encouragement, our children will do the rest.

The arts are part of what make us human. When we listen to a piece of music, watch a play or movie, or attend a dance performance, we have a chance to explore our feelings in a safe setting. We can feel joy, sadness, awe, anger, fear, etc. We can identify with the actors or dancers and see some of our own feelings acted out and see the results of those feelings in action. A performance whether it is drama, dance, or music takes us out of our usual sphere of reference and gives us a new perspective, exposing us to a larger view of the world. Visual art helps us to see something a little differently, to perhaps see a little more of the everyday world than we usually do. Art feeds our souls.

Children need to have a chance to create, perform, dance, or make music themselves. This can be at a very simple basic level as well as at a more complex and difficult level. At the same time, it's important for children to see or hear other people perform. If it's at all possible, take your children to age appropriate live arts events. They are a wonderful way to enlarge a child's world and often stimulates their own play.

Before I go any further, I'd like to take a little detour. In this chapter about the arts, I will mention my children and their accomplishments in the fields of music and art. As you read this chapter, please keep in mind that what is important is exposing your child to various artistic modes of expression not whether or not he or she becomes a "star."

I do not want you to feel as I did when I read some books about homeschooling years ago when my children were very young. I read about a 12 year old child who knit incredible sweaters for her family for Christmas. I read about very musically talented children. After reading about these children, I felt deflated and rather hopeless. I remember wondering if I had the ability to help my children achieve some sort of expertise in a field of their choosing. I also felt doubtful that my children would show any sort of talent for anything in particular. I don't think that the authors intended to create feelings of inadequacy. Instead, I think that they were just sharing their delight in their children's abilities.

As you read this chapter, please keep in mind that the information I share about my children is meant to illustrate the points I am trying to make. My children's accomplishments in the arts are not intended to be used as a ruler to measure your child's abilities. Instead, I hope that it will inspire you to explore the arts with your child. Please keep in mind that a child can enjoy music, art, dance, etc. at whatever skill level suits the child. What's important is the enjoyment, the chance to express one's self. With that said, let's move on to music.

Music

When Josh and Noah were 4½ and 2½ years old, I spent many nights worrying about how they were ever going to learn music. We lived in a small rented house that didn't have enough room for a piano nor could we afford one. I was convinced by the little bit I knew about the Suzuki method of music instruction that if they didn't start then (and perhaps it was already too late for Josh, after all he was already 4½ years old!), they would never be able to play a musical instrument. I think I was so set on the piano because I had longed to play the piano as a child. Josh is now a professional harpist. He started harp lessons when he was 13½ years old.

So why did I get so worried? I didn't do enough critical thinking about the idea that a child has to start playing a musical instrument at age 3 or 4. The adage "a little knowledge is a danger-ous thing" certainly applied to me in this situation. I wanted the best for my children. The little bit I had read about the Suzuki method seemed at the time to be the best. I did not explore other ideas about music instruction nor did I take time to look at my own experience in learning to play an instrument. Instead, I worried. I worried for about 3 months, and then accepted our circumstances and moved on to other things. (I was pregnant with Robin, our third son, at the time. One of the best things about pregnancy for me was that I found I couldn't worry for very long.)

In the intervening years, I have had time to think about music in the early years. Exposure to music is what is important. While the Suzuki Method stresses learning to play an instrument at an early age (3 to 4 years old) as well as early exposure to music, I think early exposure to music is what is vital. Children of 3 and 4 years old do not have the eye hand coordination nor the mental development to progress very fast with a musical instrument. (There are exceptions of course.) Progress often comes more readily once a child reaches the age of 8-10. Josh started playing the harp when he was 13½ years old. Robin started to play the drums and marimba when he was 12 years old. It wasn't been a handicap for either of them to have started at these ages.

It's exposure to and the experience of music in the early years that's important. That means hearing it, singing it, moving to it, clapping to it, playing it on harmonicas, kazoos, slide whistles, drums, jars with popcorn and/or beans, etc. I wish I had known this when my oldest boys were little. I wish I could go back in time and give my younger self a picture of the present. What a relief it would have been for me to know that I didn't irreparably damage my children's ability to express themselves musically because we did not start Suzuki piano lessons when Josh was 4½ years old!

Why is exposure to music in the early years important for children? Remember the "nomes" from Terry Pratchett's books that I mentioned in Chapter 1? It's hard to learn something or even imagine it exists if you've never had an experience of it. Just as we provide our children with experiences of language by reading stories and talking, we need to provide musical experiences for our children. The more music a child has had exposure to, the more familiar music will be, making it easier to learn to play music should a child choose to do so at a future date. Music has been a way that all people throughout time and in various places have expressed themselves. Music like poetry is for many children a "natural" language. Small children will sing as they play making up little tunes, especially if music has been a part of their daily lives.

The experience of listening to slow classical music has been shown to improve a person's ability to learn. "Learning improved by 24%, memory improved by 26% with the use of Baroque mu-

sic" - Iowa State University. In the book *Superlearning*, authors Sheila
Ostrander and Lynn Schroeder discuss this at great length with both
scientific studies and anecdotal stories demonstrating the effects of
listening to classical music at the largo tempo (approximately 60
beats per minute). Listening to this music has a calming effect as
well.

You may have come from a home that did not have music
or you may like a certain kind of music and know very little about
any other kind. This may make you hesitant about presenting music to your children. You might be wondering just how to get started.
I suggest that you start by singing to your babies. If it is too late for
that, sing along with various recorded music for children as you and
your children listen. Don't worry about your singing voice, just
sing along. Many adults were told when they were children that
they couldn't carry a tune. If this happened to you, sing with your
child anyway. Your child has not received the same negative programming about your voice and efforts to sing that you did. Instead your child will be pleased that you are singing - it's fun when
Mom sings along - and will join in with you.

My all time favorite children's singer is Raffi. He's a fine
musician who exudes warmth, genuine caring, and fun. The musicians that accompany him are all excellent. His many recordings
(*Singable Songs For the Very Young; More Singable Songs, Corner Grocery
Store, Rise and Shine, Baby Beluga, One Light One Sun, Raffi's Christmas
Album, Everything Grows, Bananaphone, Raffi Radio*) are great to listen
to and sing along with. He introduces different musical styles -
jazz, country and western, rock and roll, classical, etc. using children's
songs. For example, Raffi turns the song "Old MacDonald Had A
Farm" into "Old MacDonald Had a Band" introducing various
musical instruments in a delightful way.

Other singers we have enjoyed include Tom Chapin, Fred
Penner, Tom Paxton, Jessica Harper, Malvina Reynolds, and The

Travellers. Rick Scott is a spokesperson for the Down's Syndrome Foundation. He made a video of his song "Angels Do" from his CD *Philharmonic Fool* starring his granddaughter Mielle who has Down's syndrome. It's lovely and makes me cry every time I watch it. You can check his web site, www.rick-scott.com for more information.

We enjoyed singing many of the songs from a book called *Sing Through The Seasons.* They became musical staples in our house. I recorded many of those songs on a CD *Brighten the Day - songs to celebrate the seasons* in 2000. It's available from my website www.martylayne.com.

The library can be a great resource for children's music. Borrowing cassettes or CDs from the library can help you find which musicians suit your taste or strike your fancy, and then you can purchase those recordings. Please remember that musicians spent money and time to bring you their recordings. Please don't copy.

My mom sang to me when I was little. I still remember the Dutch songs and some of the poems that she taught me. One of my favorite family memories took place when I was 18 years old. My mom, my brother, my sister and I drove to Washington, D.C. We were going to meet my mother's brother who had been sent there by the German TV station he worked for. And we were going to see our grandmother, our Oma, for the first time in 10 years, and bring her home with us. I remember the songs we sang together, the harmonies we created together as we rode in the car. It was great and made the miles go faster.

I sang a lot with my children as we drove around doing errands when they were little as well as singing with them at home. Sometimes we sang along to a cassette tape but just as often we'd sing by ourselves. As everyone grew older, we sang rounds. Holly in particular enjoyed singing with me as we went to the grocery store or did other errands.

Singing doesn't have to be formal, it can be just a natural outpouring of music. Children often hum or make up songs as they play. Choirs can provide a place for your child to sing and learn some basics about music. Sometimes schools are willing to include homeschoolers in their choirs. And then there are church choirs and some communities have children's choirs. Detective work is needed to find just what will fit if your child is interested in singing in a choir.

I asked a voice professor at the University of Victoria about voice lessons for children. She said "I would recommend that a child not start formal voice training until about 13 - 14 years old when they are physically more mature. Before then choirs are great and if children want to have music lessons of some kind, encourage them to try the piano or another musical instrument."

Another way to expose your children to music is to listen to and enjoy music yourself. Josh became interested in learning to play the harp after listening to a lot of recorded Celtic harp music as he and his brothers and sister worked on a 1500 piece puzzle. My husband and I were going through a marriage crisis at the time, and both the puzzle and the music were calming for all of us. Out of that very stressful time came many positive results including Josh's interest in the harp. Everything fell into place - we found a harp for Josh and a wonderful teacher at the same time - www.joshlayne.com

A child may express an interest in learning to play an instrument after listening to music as Josh did. Sometimes a child expresses a desire to play a certain instrument seemingly out of the blue. When Robin was 12 years old, he expressed an interest in learning to play the drums. We looked around for a percussion teacher and were lucky again to find another wonderful teacher. Robin enjoyed working with his teacher as much as his teacher enjoyed working with him. We bought a drum set from our 83 year old neighbor; and Robin began practicing. It took a while to get used to the drums after hearing harp music! A few months after Robin started the drums, he began to play mallet instruments. He now plays marimba, vibes, congas, and many other percussion instruments. He's recently put together a 6 piece band to play original world beat music - Jarimba.

    I wanted to learn to play the French horn as a child, but all the school system's French horns were taken. My mom suggested the oboe instead. I had lessons through the school band and orchestra program starting when I was 10 years old. I loved the sound of the oboe and enjoyed learning how to play it.

Josh, Robin, Noah with recorders

    How can you help your child discover if he or she wants to play an instrument and if so, which one? Exposure to various instruments through recordings such as the ones I have mentioned as well as classical or other recordings like *The Orchestra* (available as a book and cassette or as a video) or the musical story *Peter and the Wolf* can help you and your child learn which instruments make which sounds.

Take your child to concerts. Some communities have orchestras or bands that offer concerts at relatively inexpensive cost, or there may be a professional orchestra in your community that offers special children's concert programs. If there's a university or college nearby with a music program, take advantage of their student recitals. They are usually free.

It's also fun to go to a music store and look at the various musical instruments, especially after listening to something like *The Orchestra*. And of course the library should have books about musical instruments with photos or other illustrations.

If your child expresses an interest in learning to play a musical instrument, finding a teacher may require some detective work on your part. If you're able to work with a your local elementary school, you may be able to be part of the school's music program and not have to pay for lessons.

If you live in a city that has an orchestra, your city more than likely also has a music conservatory or similar institution where music is taught. Talk to people in music stores, ask members of orchestras or bands for names of teachers. Before signing on with any music teacher for any length of time agree to a trial of 2 lessons to see how if this will work. Rent an instrument at first so that you and your child can see if this is an interest that your child wants to pursue. Check for special rental rates at the music stores in your area.

Holly expressed an interest in learning to play the trumpet when she was 9 years old. We rented a trumpet and found a teacher. Holly went to 2 lessons and then decided that this was not for her. We returned the trumpet and I let the teacher know that Holly would not be continuing her lessons.

The teacher was a good trumpet player, but not the right teacher for Holly. Holly and I talked at length about looking for a different teacher, but she decided that she didn't like the trumpet enough to practice as long as she knew she would need to, to make progress. She decided to join a choir and sing instead.

I sat in on Holly's two trumpet lessons, which helped me clarify for her why she wasn't happy. Her teacher did not help her to see how much she had progressed in one week. Instead, the teacher focused on what Holly needed to correct and added a few words of praise as an after thought. Knowing my daughter as I did, I knew that she had only heard the corrections.

In hindsight, I wish that I had sat in on another child's lesson to get a better idea of this teacher's teaching style, or met her in person. A telephone conversation was not enough. However, even meeting with someone may not make clear how well this particular teacher and your child will work together. I realized, too, how much more I was affected by this experience than Holly, related, I'm sure, to my own experiences with music teachers.

The teachers I had during the seven years I played the oboe were mixed. I remember how terrified I was of making mistakes. No one ever told me that every musician makes mistakes. "It's what you do between the mistakes," as Pablo Casals said, "that counts."

It may take a while to find the right teacher for your child. The work you do to find a teacher who works well with your child is well worth it. A good teacher is worth his or her weight in gold. A music teacher who enjoys teaching and is a good musician is a joy and inspiration. I hope you'll be as lucky as Josh and Robin were. They both had excellent teachers.

One of the issues that concerns many parents when their child begins to learn a musical instrument is practice times. In order to learn how to play a musical instrument, a child needs to practice. The length of time a child practices everyday is not as important as practicing everyday. Five to 15 minutes a day is adequate at the beginning. It is the everyday practice that builds skill and familiarity. It doesn't work to skip a few days and then practice 3 times as long. It's like building muscle strength, it takes place over time and can't happen all at once.

Encourage your child to practice by having a space available as well as your time available if your child wants your help. It may be helpful to discuss with your child when the practice will take place. Does your child want help to be reminded? Does your child want you to be there as he practices? Sorting out these things before hand makes this new learning activity something that you help your child with rather than something that comes between you.

Robin's self-discipline when he began to play the drums astounded me. At the beginning, he practiced about an hour a day then worked his way up to 2½ hours a day. In order for him to take part in other activities, he needed advance notification. He practiced so much because he loved it! He made very rapid progress. Robins' self-discipline stood him in good stead years later when he went to the LA Music Academy to study percussion.

Robin had Josh as an example. He heard Josh progress from 30 minutes a day of practicing to 4½ hours a day as Josh learned more and more music. Robin also watched Josh prepare for recitals and performances. He was lucky to have Josh as his live in model. To play the harp well requires lots of preparation time as it is one of the more difficult instruments to play. Robin expected that playing music well takes work.

I can remember how excited I was when I first got my oboe and began to learn to play. I practiced filled with excitement and enthusiasm. Somewhere along the line my enthusiasm became tainted by fear. I needed help from my teachers to continue to feel enthusiastic through the difficulties of mastering the oboe. Instead, I was told about the many mistakes I made. The expectations were very high, and I never felt that I would be able to meet them. The only time I was aware that I had played well was when I hadn't made any mistakes and no one hassled me. I kept playing in spite of this lack of encouragement because I loved the oboe, I loved music, and I loved making music with other people in an orchestra.

Josh's harp teacher, Kathryn Ely, did a lot to help me become aware of the negative programming I'd received about my abilities as a musician. She's an inspiring teacher. Let me give you an example. Josh was working on a piece that Nicanor Zabaleta, a well-known harpist, had recorded. Kathryn asked Josh if Zabaleta played this section faster. Josh answered, "Yes." She encouraged Josh to play it faster - "If Zabaleta did it, so can you." I would have fallen off my chair if one of my music teachers had ever said that to me. I never felt that they were on my side. Instead, I thought that I would never be good enough to please them.

Learning the skills required - the technical skills to play an instrument - is hard work. It requires practice and dedication as well as enthusiasm. It is hard to practice and improve if a child works in an atmosphere that isn't supportive, recognizing the progress being made. If you notice that your child's initial enthusiasm wanes and you are nagging your child to practice, it may be time to review what is going on for your child. It may be that the amount of work involved in learning to play an instrument is more than your child bargained for; it may be that the teacher is not the right one for your child and your child feels discouraged; or it may be something else entirely. Help your child by supporting him or her to think about what may be causing the lack of enthusiasm to practice.

If your child no longer wants to play an instrument, then

accept your child's decision and move on to another activity. This may be difficult to do because many of us have been taught that a child can't really make a decision about whether or not he likes an instrument until he's played it a while. I don't think this is true. Music comes from the heart. If a child's heart is not in it, if the heart does not sing, then the music can't come through. The work of learning to play an instrument is too hard to tackle if a child finds no joy in the process.

Two of my sons spent the better part of each day practicing their music when they were teens. Homeschooling allowed them time to explore their interest and gave them time to practice but it didn't create their talent or their love for their instruments. I wouldn't like anyone to think that because a child is homeschooled he or she will become a professional musician, professional dancer, doctor, scientist, artist, or anything else. Instead, homeschooling can give children the time to pursue their interests in depth to discover what calls to them, what makes their hearts sing. The time that a home-schooling child has to pursue an interest can reveal talent but it can't create it.

Dance - Physical Education

Just as it's important to sing to and with your child, it's important to move to music with your child. You don't have to be a great dancer or know particular steps, you just need to move to the music. Moving with your child to music encourages your child to do this on his or her own. Children are so physical. They dance with excitement or joy when something especially pleasant has happened.

Here's a suggestion using creative dance that I found useful and fun on rainy days. I put on some slow quiet music and asked my little children between the ages of 1½-5 to pretend that they were seeds planted in the ground; then to imagine that they were sprouting and slowly reaching their roots down into the earth and their first leaves up into the sun. Depending on how much my children were enjoying this and how energetic they were, there would be rain, a gentle wind or a strong wind, sun, hail, etc. until the seed had turned into a tall tree. They enjoyed this tremendously. Dance moved into drama and then back again into dance.

If you play piano, it's a great instrument to accompany this kind of creative dance. Vary the music to fit the activity - soothing for gentle rain, strident and loud for a hail storm. Sometimes my children would be the ones leading the dance and they played on the piano or a small tambourine making up music to suit the occasion, pounding hard for storms and more gently for sunshine.

Opportunities for children to learn to dance are available in most communities. One way to explore just what is available in your community and to get an overview of what a particular dance school or teacher offers is to attend an end of the year recital. These usually occur in the spring. In the fall, dance schools sometimes hold open houses where you can also learn about the types of dance instruction offered. Don't limit yourself to ballet - there are lots of different kinds of dance: clogging, folk, highland, jazz, modern, and tap to mention just a few. The advantage of going to a spring dance recital is that you and your child can see the various types of dance available in this dance school. Seeing all the different dances can help your child decide which one appeals.

Recreation centers offer dance programs as well. The advantage of a recreation center program is that they usually offer a shorter course - an 8 week session instead of an 8 month session. Talk to other parents who have their children enrolled in dance programs and ask how pleased they are with the instruction their children have received. Like with music, work on your part will be required to find a dance program and teacher to suit your child.

Like music lessons, there is often very little progress in

dance classes for small children. Ballet in particular is a very demanding form of dance and can move very slowly for small children. Your child may be just as happy dancing around on his own in your home or in the backyard.

We took folk dance classes as a family and had a great deal of fun. The other adults were thrilled to have dancers under 45 years old. We were happy because we spent the time dancing not waiting for the teachers to do crowd control.

When Holly was ready to try other forms of dance, she started taking private tap and ballet lessons with a homeschooled dancer. She soon caught up to her age peers. She moved away from home to study dance full time in a graduate dance program when she was 17. She's a professional contemporary dancer.

Dance is a physical act as well as an expressive act. Physical activity is essential for children's well being. The density of their bones when they are older is partly determined by the amount of exercise they have as children. That's why I've included physical education in this chapter. The movement of the human body is an art whether it's in dance, gymnastics, running, swimming, bowling, playing tennis, etc. Encourage your children in physical activity by doing it yourself. Go for walks, go swimming, play outdoor games like frisbee, baseball, kickball, hide and seek, etc.

If your child shows a special interest in a particular form of physical activity look for programs that will give your children skills to improve their abilities. Like looking for a music teacher or a dance program, do some talking with other parents, look around at what is available before signing up.

Keep in mind that you don't have to sign up for a program to get physical exercise. Walking to parks, jogging on trails, going swimming, playing catch, jumping rope, etc. are all things you can do with your children without instruction. One advantage to homeschooling your children is that during school hours parks, tennis courts, swimming pools, and the like are not as crowded because most children are in school. We enjoyed this calm and peaceful atmosphere in public places.

Visual Art

I mentioned the importance of having art materials available in the second chapter - paints, crayons, pencils, modeling material, and paper. When my children were younger, we did most of our art work in the kitchen. It made cleanup simpler. I encouraged my children to draw every day by taking out paper and pencils and drawing things myself. When we painted, I covered the kitchen table with newspaper, and brought out the water color paintboxes and tablets. The children would paint for an hour or so. When they were young, the artwork came from each child's imagination.

A friend gave my boys some art lessons for a few months when they were 10, 8, and 4 years old. She had them draw from life - boots, bird specimens we borrowed from the museum, still-life arrangements, etc. This was fun for them. She didn't tell them to draw any certain way, just encouraged them to look at things and try to draw them. At the time, Noah, who was 8, drew very tiny pictures. Sandra encouraged him to draw on a larger scale.

Noah continued to develop his skills by himself by looking at other artists' work, the world around him, and experimenting. Being at home allowed him time to develop his gift. He sells his work through his web site and at galleries - www.noahlayne.com.

No matter what skill level your child has, the act of creating with paint or pencil on paper is important and fun. Drawing is not only for those who are talented. It's a way of communicating no matter what the skill level involved. The Chinese proverb "One picture is worth a thousand words" is worth keeping in mind.

A child may be able to express himself in drawings and

other art work much more readily than in words. Learning to write and read depends on learning codes that may not seem very sensible to a child. That same child may be able to use a paintbrush and communicate with his own personal symbols that reveal more subtle and complex ideas and emotions than the child is capable of expressing in words. Drawing and painting comes directly from the subconscious mind and allows a child an opportunity to develop that part of himself.

Like anything, the more drawing or painting one does the greater the skill one acquires. Encourage your child to express himself in this way by providing time and materials. I sat beside my children when they were young as they drew or painted. Sometimes I'd draw or paint, too. Other times as they worked at the kitchen table, I cleaned the counters or made supper.

You might enjoy reading *Bill Peet: An Autobigraphy* to your children. Bill Peet has written many books and he used to work for Disney. Both the library and online resources are filled with ideas for children's art activities. When I set up the kitchen table for painting or drawing, I gave no instruction on how to draw or paint, unless someone asked, other than how to use the materials like a watercolor paint box and to define the rules regarding the activity (painting - on the paper not the chairs, etc.) when they painted or drew.

When we used a specific technique such as wax resist crayon drawings and black paint, I gave them an example first to demonstrate how it worked. This technique was popular at Halloween, when we drew scary pictures with crayons and then covered our pictures with black paint. It was magic to watch the paint bead up over the crayoned parts.

Another thing that's easy to use is the foam trays that come under meat or other food items for printing. Draw a picture in the foam with a pencil, then put on ink and print. There are lots of books in the library that have suggestions for art projects and techniques if you want ideas and instructions.

Origami (Japanese paper folding) is something else we have all enjoyed doing. There are many books available that come complete with instructions. See the bibliography. Paper folding leads to paper cutting and snowflakes and other folded and cut paper projects. Check the library or the internet for paper craft ideas to spark your and your child's imagination. I find it helpful to look through books to give me new ideas.

It's important to provide your child with good quality tools such as scissors that cut well and to show your children how to work safely and respectfully with these tools and other art materials. They will need supervision even after they have learned the skills. Accidents can happen so quickly. Part of teaching your children about how to use tools safely is teaching them how to call the police, fire, and/or emergency department. Even young children need to know how to call an emergency number like 911. I taught my children using dramatic play - we pretended to call 911 and acted out what would happen next.

It's also important to help children learn how to reach a parent or a family friend in case of an emergency as well as how to call the fire, police or ambulance service in your community. Basic first-aid is also useful for children to know. If you're uncertain about teaching them first-aid consider taking a course together. The Red Cross in the United States and St. John's Ambulance in Canada offer basic first-aid courses.

Display the art work that your child has created in various places, not just on the fridge. Talk with him or her about what you see using descriptive words rather than judgmental words. For example - "I see a lot of work went into this picture - there are leaves on all the branches of the trees. You have drawn the grass as individual blades, the blue of the sky is of various shades. I feel peaceful when I look at this picture. If you'd like to tell me what you were thinking of when you drew the picture, I'd like to listen." This gives your child a chance to talk about his or her art work.

Your child may or may not talk. Some children delight in sharing what they were thinking of as they made their picture. Others are focused on the act of creating and have nothing more to say. The picture expressed whatever he or she was doing and s/he may find it boring to discuss it. Using descriptive comments instead of value judgments and accepting a child's reticence to talk about his or her picture may require a lot of practice on your part.

Art galleries can be interesting, but not all children will find them so. It can be an opportunity for discussion about which art work your child did and didn't like and why or it can be a boring experience that a child wants to finish as soon as possible. Children tend to move along at various paces in a gallery. Some take a long time at each picture, others zip right through. Keep this in mind when you plan a trip to a gallery.

Picture books are also good sources of art. When my husband and I read stories to our children when they were little, we sometimes stopped reading to point out specific pictures in the books and comment about how the artist had portrayed a certain event or person. (We didn't do this all the time because it can be very disruptive to the story.) We discussed how the pictures made us feel and asked our children how they felt or what they saw. In this way we helped our children develop their visual awareness.

Taking time to notice art work in picture books, on walls in buildings, or the light shining on a tree branch gives children an experience in observing things. It encourages awareness of their surroundings and awareness of their responses to their surroundings.

As well as art to decorate the walls or tables, children can enjoy making things to decorate themselves such as items of clothing. Learning to sew, knit, crochet, or weave can all be fun. Textile arts are the source of pleasure for a number of adults. Help your children learn some of the basics so that they can discover the pleasure of these ancient crafts.

Fabric stores as well as libraries may carry beginning to sew books that have simple projects designed to teach children how to use a sewing machine. There may also be sewing courses for children offered in your communities if you don't feel comfortable teaching your child to sew. Again, take time to find out if this course and teacher will be suitable for your child.

Like music, art is a way to express one's emotions and perceptions of the world. Helping your children to express themselves artistically means helping them learn to be keen observers of the world around them and of their own internal world; to pay attention to the feelings created by certain places, sounds, smells, or sights. Encourage your children to be aware of the natural world as the seasons change or as the day turns to night. Being aware in this way, being encouraged to pay attention to these things, will give your child a wealth of experience to draw on for self-expression.

Community programs such as pottery classes, drawing classes, etc. can be a place to explore more formal artistic training. There are also artists who offer individual instruction in most communities. We have many discussions at our house whether or not anyone can teach someone else to be an artist. I think that exposure to art forms may be what is most helpful in taking classes, and the encouragement and support that these classes can provide. Make sure that any class your child takes is supportive and builds on strengths.

Dramatic Arts

Live theater captures the imaginations and takes us to another world. Live productions are magical. High schools often put on musicals or plays that are open to the public. Your local library may offer storyteller or theater events for children. Sometimes there are drama or storytelling groups that perform in elementary schools. If you've developed a good relationship with your local public school, you can ask them to let you know about any performances that will be coming to the school.

Before attending a live event, it's a good idea to do some research about the production that will be performed to see if it's suitable for the ages of your children. This goes for movies, too. If you find that the show is not suitable, it's OK to leave. Just leave as quietly as possible so that you don't disturb others.

If your child is not happy and is asking to leave, listen to your child and leave. The performers have worked hard to produce their show and the rest of the audience has come to watch the show not to listen to an unhappy child. No program is so good that it is worth having your child frightened or unhappy.

Help your child learn audience behavior by modelling this yourself - talking in the lobby rather than in the theater. I anticipated that my toddlers wouldn't be able to sit for an entire performance. I prepared ahead of time by sitting in an aisle seat so that I could go to the lobby when he or she had had enough. I could still hear the performance from the lobby even though I couldn't see it.

Some children may be interested in taking acting classes that lead to live theater productions. Like looking for dance or music teachers, do some research and watch some productions put on by any theater classes in your community. In some places, there are enough interested homeschoolers to form a drama club and put on productions.

Movies and TV shows are another source of drama. With these, like with live theater, use your discretion. As Marie Winn writes in *The Plug-In Drug,* TV can take over people's lives. We chose not to have a TV for many years. We acquired one after Noah became diabetic. Two years previously we had started a tradition of renting a TV and a VCR for a month during the time of the World Series. Being able to watch baseball games was important for Noah right after he came home from the hospital. The TV didn't change our lives as much as I thought it might. Our children preferred books to what TV had to offer.

The great thing about a VCR or DVD player is that you can control the movie or TV program you're watching. You can stop the movie, rewind it and see a sequence again, or you can stop and discuss things with each other, and then proceed. Something that's easy to do when you read to a child and is now easy to do when you watch a movie together.

Movies and plays tell us a story about people's lives - the choices they make, and how those choices effect them and their relationships with the other people in their lives. The stories in movies and plays have a strong effect because they are visual. They can transport us out of ourselves into another world, place, or time.

Stories told aloud can have that effect, too. A good story told by a good storyteller can lead a child into another world. It can be a simple retelling of an old and well known fairy tale such as "Cinderella" or "The Three Little Pigs" or it can be a brand new story that engages us.

A storyteller we've listened to for years and continue to listen to is Jay O'Callahan. He makes up the most wonderful tales and transports his listeners into his imaginary worlds. "*Herman and Marguerite* is miraculous. ...This story is practically an epic and it's about worms." - Entertainment Weekly. "Jay O'Callahan is like a prodigious one-man band in his ability to single-handedly create a cast of characters and set rich and complex scenes." - Parents' Choice Award. Look for his recordings in your local library or go online to *ocallahan.com* to check out his extensive list of recordings for both children and adults.

We enjoyed each of his stories. They became a part of our lives. Key phrases from his stories still appear in our own conversations to illustrate points - "Give him a pickle to quiet him down." or "It's a good game. It's a good game." Jay tells stories for older listeners, too. His stories about his own growing up years are wonderful. He was commissioned by the town of Bethlehem, PA to write a story about steel -*Pouring the Sun*. His stories are unique and wonderful.

Conclusion

As a society we pay lip service to the idea that every person on the earth comes with special gifts, but we tend to recognize only outstanding gifts that fall in recognized categories like art, music, dance, drama, or sports. We are not willing to recognize talent for something like happiness, listening to others, being a warm-person, taking delight in a rainy day, etc.

It's important to remember that the uniqueness of your child may not fall into a recognized category. There's a woman I think of frequently when I think of our hero worship of "stars." This woman worked in the local post office when my children were young. She had a gift for creating peace. During pre-Christmas lineups, her talent for recognizing each person, making eye contact, and speaking calmly was a real treasure. When my turn would come, her warmth and good humor would fill my depleted reservoir of patience and I'd leave feeling so much better. I saw this happening to others in the line as well.

Her gift doesn't fall into a recognized category nor would she be publicly acknowledged in any way, yet she made a difference to her customers. Twenty five years later I still think of her, thankful for our encounters.

In this chapter I've tried to show you how important the arts are for your child, not because the arts may be come a profession but because the process of creation/play is vital to their well being. I think we were born to create - be it a poem, a garden, a song, a pleasant space, a drawing, a cake, a dance, etc. The form isn't as important as the doing, the creating.

Homeschooling allows children time to pursue creative activities. My children's creative activities were the source of their education. In the process of play - dramatic, physical (like sports), musical, or artistic - they learned about the world, people, animals, plants, etc. Encourage and support your children by providing materials, space, your attention, new points of view, live performances by both amateurs and professionals, discussions, teachers (when needed), descriptive comments about their creations, and your sincere appreciation of their efforts.

Robin

CHAPTER 7
Life As Curriculum

When I was in high school in a suburb of Chicago from 1962-1966, I assumed that what I was being required to learn to graduate and become an "educated" person was the standard and complete body of knowledge for all high schools across the U.S., that anyone with a high school diploma would know the same things that I knew. I've found out since that my assumption was incorrect.

I've asked my friends (who were in high school during the 60's, 70's, and 80's in both the United States and Canada) and my husband (who was in high school in the 60's in Louisville, KY) about their high school educations. What they learned didn't coincide with what I'd learned. I expected that there would be some difference, but the differences were much greater than I expected. These differences tell me that what I had been led to believe as being absolutely essential to know wasn't necessarily so. These differences helped me to see that an educated person is defined by the cultural values of time and place.

As I described the way in which I helped my children with reading, writing and math in the previous chapters, you probably noticed that I didn't follow a set curriculum or use textbooks. Our curriculum was based on whatever interests my children had. Using these interests, I helped them gain a mastery of what I consider to be the skills necessary for living in the world today. These include being able to read fluently and with pleasure, write fluently, understand arithmetic well enough to balance a checkbook, learn how to manage money, understand basic nutrition to maintain health, learn how to pursue an idea or project, and learn to think critically and imaginatively. Because the body of material an educated person is expected to learn and know shifts with time and cultural bias, my goal was to help my children become competent in the skills listed above so that they could use these skills to acquire any information or knowledge as needed throughout their lives..

In the book *If You Want to Be Rich and Happy, Don't Go to School*, the author, Robert T. Kiyosaki, discusses the importance of being a generalist. He emphasizes how disabling it can be to be trained in only one subject and not understand how to go about acquiring new training or information that one might need particularly after a job loss. Learning how to acquire information has been the main focus of our homeschooling.

Before going any further, let me go to my dictionary again. *The New Lexicon Webster's Encyclopedic Dictionary of The English Language Canadian Edition* defines curriculum as " a course of study, esp. at school or college; a list of the courses offered at a school, college, or university [Latin = a running race]"

Just as we didn't use textbooks for reading, writing, or math, we didn't for science, history, or geography. Instead, we followed interests as our curriculum or course of study. It's only in the world of academics that separate fields of study exist.

Separate fields of study are a convenience to make the amazing chaos and beauty of life on our planet somewhat more understandable from our human point of view. Fields of study can be a useful way to learn but it is important to keep in mind that this separation is a created convenience and only describes a portion of the whole. Fields of study, like dissection, divide up the whole, and the whole is often more than the sum of its parts.

With this in mind, let's explore some of the ways you can use your every day experiences to the fullest and enable your children to have a richer appreciation and understanding of the wonderful complexity of life. Let's take making a salad for example. Let me show you how making a salad can cover biology, sociology, physiology, geography, chemistry, language arts, and meteorology.

We had some interesting discussions about lettuce as we made salads (language arts), e.g., where and how it is grown (geography, chemistry, biology, agricultural practices). In the summer, we picked it out of the garden which led to discussions about bugs and slugs. Because we garden organically and do not use pesticides, we tended to have slugs in our lettuce. One day at supper, we were discussing slugs and I had an opportunity to relate the way I used to trap slugs when I lived in Cape Breton, Nova Scotia as a self-sufficient farmer. We discussed the difference in climate between Victoria, where we live, and Cape Breton (meteorology). I related how I had used beer in little plastic dishes to attract the slugs. The slugs would crawl in attracted by the beer, and then drown in the beer (biology). This then led to a discussion of alcoholic beverages and why people drink them (sociology).

Baseball was often a major topic of discussion in our house. The boys used to keep track of the batting averages of many players (statistics). They read about baseball players in the newspaper and kept track of the salaries earned (economics), the drugs some players use (sociology, human physiology), the trades that are made (statistics and strategic thinking). Each of them knew where the cities were that have major league baseball teams (geography). They had a great store of information about which team won which pennant when (history). They knew the differences between knuckleballs and fast balls (physics) and the consequences of certain injuries for a player's future ability to play (human physiology, economics).

We had discussions about the high salaries players receive at such young ages (psychology, economics); the process of resolving the baseball strike of 1994 (sociology, psychology, history). When they were 17 and 15 years old, Josh, Noah and I watched a film, *Bingo Long and The Travelling All Stars*, about an African American baseball team and the beginning of integration in sports and discussed it (African American studies, history, race relations).

I'm sure that once you start, you can find similar opportunities in your family's life for discussion and exploration that will broaden everyone's understanding. Homeschooling your child gives you many opportunities to engage your children in this sort of discussion. When a child is particularly intrigued by an aspect of life, say horses, you can use that subject as your curriculum. You can go to see actual horses, perhaps give your child an opportunity to ride. You can learn with your child all about the history of horses and the various breeds. This can be done both through nonfiction and fiction books.

Sometimes, fictional accounts of people and their relationships with horses are more meaningful than just reading a list of facts about horses. Books like *Misty of Chincoteague* by Margeruite Henry give a child a glimpse of what it's like to have a pony and train her. If you go to the library, you can find many other books about the subject of horses that you can read together. You can start this at any age a child shows interest in a particular area. Read books aloud so that you, too, learn more about the subject your child is interested.in. .

Science

Because I have four children, I had the opportunity to learn about a lot of things that I would not necessarily have chosen to learn on my own as I helped them pursue their own interests. At the same time, they participated in my interests and had hands-on experiences with gardening when they were younger.

Josh and his pumpkin

Much of the information my children learned from me in the field of science was related to gardening, animals, and health. We dug in the dirt and observed the bugs, the consistency of the soil, the size of the rocks, and the smell of the soil. We spent time observing how the seeds grew into plants, which birds came to the garden, and how fast things grew. This was done as we worked in the garden, as we prepared a meal, or as we went on walks.

When my two older boys were 7 and 5 years old they were fascinated by magnets, electricity, how fast things went, and magic tricks. We visited electronics shops and stocked up on the basics: wires, batteries and battery holders, little light bulbs and holders, and small electric motors so that they could learn about how circuits worked. They did lots of experiments on their own, figuring out how to follow diagrams and how to design their own circuits.

They also enjoyed experiments with vinegar and baking soda.

Although this could have been an opportunity for me to explain chemical formulas and how a base and an acid interact to produce gas, I didn't. I had a 2 year old to look after, and could only do so much. Josh and Noah were happy with the basic explanation I gave them and just enjoyed observing the effect. If they'd been really keen on understanding this more thoroughly, they would have continued to ask questions because they did at other times when they wanted more information.

I want to stress how easy it can be to use a child's interest as your curriculum. A child who is fascinated by dinosaurs can learn a lot about many fields of study as well as learn about reading, writing and math. Pacing out just how big a Tyrannosaurus Rex was, is a fun way to do math. Drawing pictures of what the world may have looked like when there were dinosaurs can help children be aware of the food cycle, etc. In other words, if you start anywhere, you will find many layers and side paths to explore that will lead you and your child in all sorts of interesting directions and cover many fields of study.

At the same time that you encourage your children's interests, you don't have to use every question or interest as a "teachable moment." In fact, it's impossible to do this. It would drive everyone crazy. My children made it fairly obvious when they wanted to know more and when they'd had enough. "Stop, Mom, we just want to play."

You may feel that you're not knowledgeable enough to help your child pursue various interests in the field of science. As I mentioned in previous chapters, you don't have to teach you children everything yourself when you homeschool. If your child has an interest that you know very little about and you have no interest in learning anymore about, look for someone who does have that knowledge and ask this person to work with your child. Instructors are often quite surprised by the self-motivation of homeschooled children.

You can participate by helping your child learn to evaluate the experience. One way to do this is to describe to your child what you see as the child gets ready for this activity or while the child is engaged in the activity. "When you get ready to go riding, you're always ready 15 minutes early, eagerly waiting. You must really like riding." or "You seem to go inside yourself when it's time to go riding. You're not smiling. How are you feeling about riding?"

Learning to evaluate an activity to see if it's still suitable is an important lifelong skill. To be able to assess the pros and cons of a situation and determine if it is of value is useful for a child and even more useful for an adult. I mentioned something about this in the last chapter in regard to practicing a musical instrument. Learning about one's likes and dislikes, one's goals, and one's hopes helps a child begin to set priorities. With experience in evaluating activities, children gain an understanding of themselves, useful when making career choices.

Moving back to the subject of curriculum - with the understanding that anything can be used as your curriculum - following your child's interests gives you a core curriculum or course of studies. If the passion for information about dinosaurs changes, you can use the next interest in the same way. Your child hasn't lost anything by changing interest, instead, he gained an understanding of the world of dinosaurs. Both of you will gain further knowledge as other interests are pursued.

As an example of living everyday science, our pets have been a great way to learn about zoology. We've had gerbils, parakeets, cats, guinea pigs, rabbits, chickens, and a goldfish. We had five cats - two mothers and three of their daughters, for 15 - 18 years. We found it fascinating to watch the interaction of our cats and their different personalities. When two of our cats had kittens, we enjoyed watching the kittens grow. Holly was only three at the time, but she can still remember watching one of them be born.

Taking care of our various pets meant learning about them - their natural habitat; their reproduction cycle; their natural predators; their natural diet; their ways of dealing with shock, trauma, or injury; and their responses to human interaction.

If at all possible, include some sort of pet in your family life. Guinea pigs are fairly easy to take care of and can easily be kept in a cage indoors. Their living quarters need to be cleaned regularly, so a child will need help to clean and change the bedding. Check at the library or a pet store to find out the housing requirements for any pet you intend to add to your home. Do the research required so that you know what you're getting into.

If you acquire a pet, you will need to help your child learn how to handle the pet gently. You will need to help your child learn how to take care of a pet. Children under 7 years old cannot be expected to regularly feed and take care of pets. They will need assistance. It is unfair for an animal to suffer because a child is not able to be a responsible caretaker at all times. You will need to be willing to ensure that a pet receives proper care and attention. You'll also have to take care of injuries that may happen. As your child grows older, he or she will be more able to take over all of the care and feeding of a pet.

Taking care of a live animal can be a delight for a child. Pets can bring children tremendous joy. There is something wonderfully soothing about stroking an animal. An animal can give a child a gift of love and affection, and a child can give love, affection, and care to an animal. This gives a child a sense of importance, of mattering to another living being.

Something else to consider when thinking about getting a pet is that pets die. It's important to help your child deal with the grief they will experience when a pet dies. There are many books about death and dying (these are written about people but can be useful in the death of a pet) that may help you at a time like this. Death brings up many questions about life and its purpose. What you do to help your child if a pet dies, helps both of you to come to a better understanding of your particular belief system. If a child is supported as he grieves, than the hurt of the loss passes and healing takes place. Some people offer the well meaning advice that as soon as a pet dies, replace the pet with another one. I think it's important for a child to have time to feel the loss. The loss is there and real whether or not we are willing to recognize it. Unlike broken toys, pets are not interchangeable. Take time after the death of a pet to allow your child to grieve.

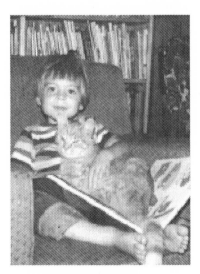

Robin with Elf

Holly with Cuddles

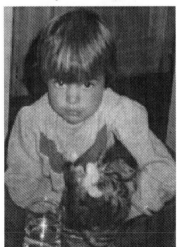

What to do if a child shows no particular interest

So what happens if your child expresses no particular interest? Then you might need to try reading lots of different stories about lots of different people and situations. You might need to listen to lots of different kinds of music. You might need to explore your natural environment together and talk together to see if there isn't something that intrigues your child.

At certain times, it seems as though there is nothing that interests a child. A child who was busy and content suddenly becomes bored and grumpy. I think these stages in a child's life are related to physical growth spurts, particularly ages 10-12. Everything may seem boring to your child. This is a difficult time for both you and your child and it is a normal state of development.

It is almost as though a child is discarding everything that used to be fun or exciting in order to make room for new ideas and interests, yet those new interests are not always as quick to appear as the boredom with the old. I wish I had a quick fix answer. This is a time when you must work hard to maintain a relationship with your child free from blaming him/her for this state as well as free of accepting the blame for your child's boredom (as long as you have done your part by providing a stimulating learning environment for your child - see Chapter 2). Your child needs to know you are available and supportive but that at a certain point in his life you are unable to make his dissatisfaction go away.

This dissatisfaction is a natural phenomenon - like rain and sunshine. It is also like the stage of labor in childbirth called transition. During this transition stage of labor, I felt, as many women have, that I would rather not have a baby after all. I felt like saying "Let's just forget the whole thing." Intellectually, I knew about this stage which helped me because I was aware that it would happen, but it didn't change the fact that I needed to go through the stage and experience it. Between contractions, I would remember that I had done this before and the pushing part would come soon, leading to a baby being born. I could hardly wait to get to the pushing part. However during a contraction I would forget and I wanted to stop and not have a baby after all. Perhaps, if you could think of yourself as a labor coach for your child as he or she goes through the transitions of physical growth spurts, it might make it easier for both of you.

One of the most important things to remember when you're homeschooling is that your children will not be happy, busy, self-motivated learners all the time. That's impossible. It's normal and expected that children will be unhappy or lonely or bored. When they are young and express their boredom in unacceptable physical ways, it might be a good time to go for a walk, a run, a swim, or a change of locality - such as going outside - change activities and read them a story. As they grow older, you can share with them what you do when you are bored, lonely, or angry, how you cope when you feel as they do.

As I said before, there is no easy, quick-fix solution to this situation. What is required is time and patience. Keep reading stories, keep talking to your child, offer to help explore other possibilities, and accept that there will be difficult times. However, as stated in Chapter 2, a child needs to understand that the expression of his or her unhappiness needs to be respectful of others.

I hope that the examples I have used to illustrate "Life as Curriculum" are helpful. Keep in mind that not all homeschoolers are as unstructured about curriculum as I was. Many use textbooks to guide their studies. There is a wealth of material available to help you find curriculum both in books, magazines, and online.

No matter how homeschooling takes place, one of the benefits of homeschooling is that a child has control over time in a different way than a child in school. If a certain topic is of great interest, than the child can pursue it without being told that "The period is

over. Time to start another subject." One of the other benefits is
the companionship of their parents and siblings.

Here is a list of a few books with a scientific slant that I
found helpful as we explored the world around us.

Bet You Can and *Bet You Can't* by Vicki Cobb. Both of these
books have fun science tricks that our children enjoyed doing. Vicki
Cobb has written a number of books about the science of everyday objects that you may find interesting. Her website has lots of
info and links that look like fun www.vickicobb.com.

The Magic School Bus books by Joanna Cole illustrated by
Bruce Degen. The stories take place in a classroom as the children
study different science topics with Miss Frizzle their teacher. My
favorite is *The Magic School Bus at The Waterworks*. The children become as small as raindrops and participate in the whole cycle of
how water is carried to people's homes and then used and recycled.
(There's a Tom Chapin song "The Wheel of the Water" on his
recording *Mother Earth* that describes this process in song.) This
book and the others in the series impart information with humor.
We enjoyed these as picture books when my children were quite
young. As they grew older, they still enjoyed the books, retaining
more information because of their age and greater experience.

Eyewitness Juniors - a whole series of books on Amazing Mam-
mals, Birds, Snakes, Spiders, etc. Good illustrations, both drawings
and photographs and lots of facts in small paragraphs in various
places on the page. Good for children 4-5 years old as well as older
ones who can read on their own and enjoy learning about animals.
Available in paperback, published by Alfred A. Knopf.

Harper and Row publishes a whole series of I-Can-Read
Science books that most libraries carry in their primary reading section. One of our favorites was *Benny's Animals* by Millicent Selsam.

Show your children where the nonfiction books are kept in
the library and how to find those subjects that especially interest

them. Help them to feel comfortable browsing through both the fiction and nonfiction sections of the library.

The main thing to keep in mind as you homeschool your child is that your curiosity sets a model for your child. If you enjoy learning new things or exploring new ideas, your child more than likely will, too. You need to be honest and only show an interest if you actually have an interest in a subject. I bought electrical equipment to make it possible for my boys to explore how circuits worked, but I didn't participate in their experiments beyond the basics. They explored on their own. Talking about our cats or about plants was different. Animal and gardening topics are easy for me to be enthusiastic about. However, when one of my children showed a particular interest in something, I helped him or her find resources to explore this interest even if I didn't share it.

What's important when homeschooling is to be able to support your child genuinely in his own interests. If that interest is not one you can share, find someone else who can. Teachers' associations may have a list of unemployed teachers who are available for tutoring. It can be a very rewarding relationship for both child and tutor if you can find someone who's enthusiasm is genuine and with whom your child enjoys working. By finding others who can help your child pursue an interest, you show your child that you respect and support the child's need for knowledge and information beyond your expertise.

Think of Gerald Durrell (whom I mentioned in Chapter 2) as an example. His family was not knowledgeable about natural history, but they either supported or tolerated his interest. Each of the members of his family had certain passions in life. It was accepted and expected. As an adult, he continued his passion for animals and became a collector of rare and almost extinct animals. He established breeding programs for them in his own zoo, The Jersey Trust. One of the ways he raised funds for his zoo was through writing about his life as a child in Corfu and his life as a collector of animals. His books are great read alouds for older children, filled with humorous anecdotes about his family and lots of natural history information about animal life.

I hope this very brief look at science is helpful and gives you some ideas. From my point of view, observation and sharing one's observations are the foundations of science study. Children learning at home have many opportunities to observe the world around them as well as many opportunities to manipulate objects and observe the effects of those manipulations. Like with mathematics, science is often defined by vocabulary. Science is a part of life and doesn't have to be studied divorced from life.

Some children may show a particular interest in a branch of science that may need special nurturing by you or someone else. One of the benefits of homeschooling is that a child with a particular interest can have time to pursue it.

To close this section on science let me quote from the forward of *Absolute Zero Gravity: A collection of jokes, anecdotes, and riddles, revealing the funny side of physics, biology, mathematics and other branches of science* by Betsy Devine and Joel E. Cohen: "Scientists are funny people. Not just the great ones who think they have discovered the secret of life or of the brain or of the common cold. Even ordinary day-to-day scientists are funny, because they all think that the world makes sense! Most people know better."

Social Studies

As with science, I used opportunities as they arose to bring history and geography into our lives. Family history was our starting place as my children liked hearing stories about when I was younger or stories about their father's and grandparents' lives. I used stories almost exclusively to present historical information.

There is something so appealing in stories. As Robert Coles, author of *The Call of Stories* (and many other books) says "It is the perspective, the morality, the way in which people view the information of their lives that give things meaning." (He taught literature courses at Yale Medical and Law School to introduce future doctors and lawyers to some of the ethical questions of their professions through situations presented in literature.)

I've learned more social studies through reading stories than any other method. Stories have been used for thousands of years to educate. Before we had the printed word, we had stories. Stories were the way people remembered where they came from, who they were as a people, how to live their lives, and when it was time to do the things that needed to be done. Stories have given people pleasure, taught valuable lessons, and given spiritual succor for ages.

Reading aloud to my children went from picture books which told stories about people and places, some imaginary some real, to longer chapter books about both real and imaginary people.

As the books became longer, the issues they presented became more complex. We covered a lot of historical ground by reading books by authors who have written historical fiction for children: Ian Serralier, Kate Seredy, Rosemary Sutcliffe, Geoffrey Trease are a few authors whose work we read and enjoyed. The stories I read my children brought us in touch with many cultures, many historical periods, and many people's lives. As we read, we took time to discuss the characters, their actions, decisions, and thoughts. These characters became our friends, a part of our lives. (In retrospect, I realize that I did more of the work of homeschooling at bedtime - reading stories, discussing stories, or discussing other matters my children brought up - than at any other time of the day.)

Let me give you an example. I read a series of three books to Holly when she was 10 years old by Bernice Hunter about a girl named Margaret who goes to live with her aunt and uncle, *A Place for Margaret, Margaret In The Middle, Margaret On Her Way.* The series takes place in Ontario, Canada during the 1930s. It presents a detailed picture of life in a large family during the Depression years. I then read *Cheaper by The Dozen* and *Belles on Their Toes* to both Holly and Robin, also about a large family during the same time period but in the United States. As a result of these stories, Holly and I had some very interesting discussions about families and how mothers and children relate to each other.

Holly very astutely observed that if a mother wasn't breastfeeding her baby anybody could take care of that baby. She also wondered when women stopped nursing their babies and why. We discussed the Industrial Revolution and how that affected mothers and babies. We talked about the change from an agrarian economy to an industrial economy. I was pleased and surprised by Holly's perception that artificial infant feeding has a great impact on a mother and child's relationship.

I loved these discussions. They were a forum for critical thinking. They provided an opportunity for my children to express their thoughts and share their perceptions. Discussing the characters in a story gave us a chance to talk about values, goals, and moral choices. It gave us a chance to talk about how people in different times and places made decisions.

Stories give perspective and help us to see the world through another person's point of view. Stories can help put facts in a framework. *The Little House Books* by Laura Ingalls Wilder are a good example: she brings to life the experiences of the pioneers moving West. I've read this series of books aloud three times to various groupings of my children. As I read them aloud, I took time to share my reactions to some of the things "Ma" said. We discussed how differently "Pa" and "Ma" related to their children, etc. We enjoyed the glimpse into the events of Laura's childhood. We were also aware of how differently people thought at that time, e.g., Ma saying she "Didn't like to go to the store for every little thing."

Some of those ways of thinking irritated me - "Ma's" dislike of Indians or the total subservience of women to men. Some of the incidents that described the behavior expected of men and women at the time helped me to gain a better understanding of some of our present day difficulties. I discussed my reactions and thoughts with my children. They enjoyed telling me what they thought about what a character said or did. I connected an incidents in a story to our own personal family history - for example - "Grandma was born about the same time as so and so in this story." This helped us to have a new understanding of Grandma.

Roger Lee McBride wrote a series of books about Laura's daughter Rose that continues the story of Laura and her family. Holly and I thoroughly enjoyed them. There are now books available about Caroline, Laura's mother, written by Maria D. Wilkes; stories about Charlotte who is Caroline's mother and Laura's grandmother by Melissa Wiley; and Martha who is Charlotte's mother, Caroline's grandmother, and Laura's great-grandmother by Melissa Wiley, published by Harper Trophy. An interesting way to look back over five generations.

We also enjoyed the series of books about a girl named Anastasia Krupnik (and that's the title of the first book in the series) by Lois Lowry. They describe life in the 1970's and 80's. They're great read alouds and quite funny. I have read them aloud twice and wouldn't mind reading them aloud a few more times. Lois Lowry captures the character of Anastasia so well starting when Anastatia is 10 and up through her 13th year.

The discussions that we had were as important as the story. We discussed how these characters made decisions. This gave us an opportunity to explore how we make decisions and a chance to look at our values. This type of discussion is vital. It gives children a chance to practice discretion, discernment, and judgment. We are bombarded with information and choices everyday. How do we decide which piece of information to use when we make a decision? How do we judge the accuracy or the application of a certain fact to our situation?

We need the wisdom that stories contain. We often have more than enough information. What we need help with is how to sort that information so that it can be useful in our lives. We need the works of fiction, fairy tales, and myth because they address the age old questions of mankind. The outer circumstances have changed and more often than not we do not have something as easily visible as a dragon to fight, but the inner struggles of our lives remain the same.

My children heard enough fairy tales to know the structure of a fairy tale. They were aware of the various twists and turns that happen in such a tale. For example, the old woman whose nose is stuck in a tree on the path to your destination may be more important than the destination. Fairy tales and myths reach beyond our intellectual understanding to a deeper place within us. Like art and music, they reach into our souls.

Stories can serve to guide us when we experience struggles and trouble in our lives. We can turn to stories of people or children in difficult circumstances and draw strength from their survival. Stories about how children coped during World War II were important for Noah when he was about 9 years old. *The Silver Sword, The Chestry Oak, The House of Sixty Fathers,* and *Number the Stars* inspired him because they were filled with children's courage. These stories and others like them help us to see our own suffering and worries, our lives, in a larger context. And isn't that the point of history?

Taking a detour from the topic of history, I want to mention that while I have used my children's interests as a starting point for some of our reading, exploring, etc., I have not blindly followed their interests. I think about the 8 year old girl who was killed in an airplane crash in 1996 while flying the plane with her instructor and father present. They were trying to establish a record of some sort and took off in inclement weather. The girl's mother was quoted in my local paper as stating that flying was something her daughter loved to do and she wouldn't keep her from it. I want to be clear that in helping your child follow his or her interests, you need to use your discretion.

I spoke about safety in Chapter 2 - creating a safe space both physically and emotionally. If a child is not allowed to drive a car before reaching the age of 16, why was a child flying an airplane at age 8? Children of that age have barely developed the cones and rods in their eyes necessary to see peripherally to cross the street safely. How could a child of that age be able to sort out all the factors needed to fly an airplane?

This is an important issue. As a parent it is your responsibility to protect your children from harm. We need to work carefully to create a safe path for our children to walk as they pursue their interests. We want them to reach adulthood! Encouraging your child to pursue his interests doesn't mean that you must do whatever the child wants. It means using a child's interests as a way to learn about the world. It means finding and then doing age appropriate or developmentally appropriate activities in the field of interest. I can't emphasize enough how important it is to use your discretion - to develop your powers of discernment so that you can guide your children as they learn.

I hope that this chapter has given you some ideas to use to explore the different interests and ideas your children have. Science and social studies are a window, a point of view on life. They do not define life. Learning at home can offer an opportunity for an inter-disciplinarian way of learning that is limited only by your imagination.

A good example of an inter-disciplinarian way of looking at life is *The Day the Universe Changed* available on DVD. James Burke takes a number of turning points in history such as the development of movable type and shows some of the events that led up to that particular turning point and the repercussions this event has had on the present. (There is an accompanying book that I find helps me to remember what he's said.) He combines science, history, art, music, philosophy, etc. to explore these events. A great example of life as curriculum. The series is adult oriented. I wouldn't recommend it for children under 13, mainly because I don't think younger children would find it very interesting. He does a lot of talking. Of course, you are the best judge of your children's interest and ability to understand and may find that you have a child who is quite intrigued with the program. My two oldest boys found it a fascinating series to watch. It fit right into the way they learned about science and social studies - in context with other events.

I've listed some books and authors that I found helpful within the text of this chapter. There is also a list of authors in the bibliography for this chapter, including the ones I mentioned. Use your library and librarians as resources to flesh out a topic by providing titles for related fiction and nonfiction books. If you use life as your curriculum, you have the whole world available as subject matter.

We're in the midst of a turning point in regard to education. At one time education was a scarce commodity, a privilege for those who had wealth and it was tied to a certain locality. With the development of electronic communication, personal computers, and the internet, information is no longer scarce nor is it as privileged. The effects of this will be hard for us to see for many years. Just as it was hard for those alive during the time of the printing of the *Guttenberg Bible* to predict what effect movable type would have on their society. Anyone can learn almost anything with computer access. Children learned at home in the past. An ever growing number of children learn at home in the present. It will be very interesting to see how technology and access to information interact with education in the future.

Making apple cider

Life with a 3 year old and a baby

CHAPTER 8
Burn-out

The stress of mothering is enormous in our North American culture. Add to that the challenge of homeschooling, and the potential for burn-out is great. In this chapter, you'll find my thoughts about the causes of burnout, ideas and thoughts about recognizing the signs of burnout, and some suggestions about what to do when feeling overwhelmed and burned-out.

I think that the main source of burnout and stress is conflict. Although conflict is a normal part of life and it can be a great force for action and change, when we are faced with conflict very few of us are comfortable with it. When that conflict is internal conflict, our discomfort increases and our ability to function decreases. Inner conflict can help us to rethink our present attitudes, decisions, or actions. Yet, if we are subject to constant inner conflict, we become overloaded and our circuits burnout.

Learning how to resolve conflict is vital to successful homeschooling. For me resolving conflict has meant looking at my conflict in the light of my philosophy of education (of life). This takes a lot of work. However, once I've done the work and resolved a particular conflict, life seems to flow more smoothly until another conflict comes along.

Mothering in and of itself can be rife with inner conflict; "Should I be cleaning the house right now, I have a few minutes while everyone is busy? Should I go and find Suzie and read her a story like I said I would? Should I take a few minutes and just sit down and have a cup of tea?" Experienced mothers talk about how often they think perhaps they ought to be doing something other than what they're doing. For new mothers, this constant confusion of what should be done can be as draining as the change in sleep patterns that a new baby brings. Add homeschooling to the load and you add an infinite number of shoulds to the mix.

I've found that one of the most important things for me to do to prevent that crash is to limit my sources of both external and internal conflict. When I found myself caught up in conflict, it helped me to look at the problem in terms of needs. Here's an example. When Noah was struggling to learn to read at age 9, much of my panic and inner conflict had to do with other people's expectations. They'd tell me that a child should learn to read by at least 6, 7, 8 years old or "He's just being lazy and won't read because you read everything to him. You should make him read it himself." I questioned myself and began to doubt my philosophy of education and my perceptions of the situation. I wondered if I was doing Noah a disservice by not pushing him, but when I looked, I saw that I was already pushing him beyond his limits.

My need to have Noah read at age 9 because of pressure from others was in conflict with my need to respect my child's development. Other people's concern confused me. I wondered how to balance their concern, my need to defend myself, Noah's developmental stage, and my philosophy of education. As Noah struggled to learn to read, he began to feel incompetent. He was doing his best and he wasn't ready to read. I switched the problem around. Noah didn't have the problem, it belonged to me. He wasn't developmentally ready. I didn't need him to read to prove that I was capable. I backed off. I still worried from time to time, but I would remind myself of why I had made the decision and wait. Eventually, he learned to read.

When Holly turned 9, she, like Noah, wasn't ready or able to read the way her brothers Josh and Robin did when they were 9 years old. Holly and I worked together on reading at various times as I wrote about in Chapter 3, but I was not anxious the way I was with Noah. I knew that eventually Holly would learn to read fluently and with pleasure, which she did. I could accept her pace. I was not caught up in the same inner conflict as I had been with Noah.

I've used this particular example to illustrate how important it is for you to take a close look at what is causing you conflict. Take time to explore your expectations for your child as well as your expectations of yourself. Often, we have a number of hidden expectations, hidden agendas that can cause tremendous turmoil especially if they stay hidden.

When I'm in a conflicting situation, I remind myself to think of the stages of labour in childbirth. Most women have expectations of how labor will proceed. We have dreams of the birth of our new baby. However, sometime during the labor we are confronted by the reality of this particular birth and this particular baby. When we can let go of our intellectual control and go with the wisdom of our bodies in the process of labor, birth happens more easily.

Working with our children when helping them learn is similar to this. Quite often we are called on to reevaluate our belief system and take a close look at our child and see how we can best meet this child's needs. We are also called on to have the courage to face our fears about our ability to help our children learn as well as our children's abilities. If we can do all of this with gentleness and patience, often a shift takes place and resolution is born. It is often not quite what we expected. There is no answer already defined waiting for us. We have to develop and find our own answers. This takes time and can be very draining while at the same time it can be tremendously energizing to make these kinds of changes. The book *Expecting Adam* by Martha Beck is a wonderful example of the kind of change I mean. Martha Beck wrote this book about her experiences when she was pregnant with her son, Adam, who has Down's syndrome.

As we sort and sift through our thoughts, our children's needs and abilities, our concerns, we can be in constant turmoil, wondering which decision to make and hoping that it is not the wrong one. Perhaps it might help you to know that everyone who homeschools makes mistakes. (Actually, all parents make mistakes. It's what we do with the mistakes when we recognize them that's the important thing. Mistakes are the way we learn.) Most homeschooling mothers question the wisdom of many of their decisions. We are trying something new and have old models for how to do this. One of the problems for many of us in trying this new way of educating our children is that when we went to school we learned that making mistakes was not acceptable. We feel uncomfortable when we make mistakes. We expect perfection of ourselves. We want to score 100% in terms of doing the right things with our children.

Unlike taking a test, homeschooling a child does not come with such clearly defined right answers. You are the one who determines what those right answers are. As in any new situation, we are like nestling birds on their first flight, we will fall for a while before we learn how to use our wings and start our upward ascent. I hope reading about my experiences in this book will help you to find your wings a little sooner.

If you find yourself in constant conflict, accept the conflict and take time to sort out what the issues are. As I mentioned in Chapter 1, the book *People Skills* by Robert Bolton has a section about conflict and problem solving that I found helpful. Although he doesn't use examples of inner conflict, they are interpersonal, I found that the techniques can be applied to inner conflict as well as external conflict.

Interpersonal conflict can also be a tremendous drain and cause burnout. You may find that you and your spouse and/or partner do not see eye to eye about how to go about homeschooling. It's important to take time to work on this and find some way that you can agree to disagree at the very least. You may need to consult with someone who can facilitate communication between you to help you and your partner work things out. Be aware that some people who do this kind of couples' work may have strong feelings about homeschooling and may have a vested interest in the outcome. They may not be able to be neutral about homeschooling.

You may find that you and your child are in constant conflict. Teaching is an art. It requires a gentle touch and a great deal of willingness on the part of the teacher to figure out how to help a particular person learn. As the adult in the relationship, it is up to you to find a way to solve the conflict.

The conflict that you may be experiencing with your child could be the difficulty of being both teacher and mother. A teacher in school can assign a child to write an essay or do so many pages of math and check the next day to see that it is done. As a home-schooling mother, you do not have the distance that a teacher has. You will be there as your child does this work. If your child is not willing to do this work, you need to use a lot of your energy and patience to help your child complete the work you have assigned. You play two roles, the supportive mother and the demanding teacher. Your child may be angry at you for being a task master, and this may be difficult for both of you.

Some homeschooling families solve this by using correspondence courses. Assignments come from a teacher so the mother and teacher roles are kept separate.

Using the "Life as Curriculum" approach as I did, there was no separation between the teacher and mother role. The work that I asked my child to do had an impact on my relationship with that child. I therefore weighed the necessity of that work against the necessity of maintaining a positive relationship with my child.

Some children take suggestions more readily than others. Some children welcome constant help, others want to be left alone to work things out for themselves. It will take time and patience on your part to find the best way to work with your child. You have already learned a lot about your child as he or she moved through his/her baby and toddler years. You can build on what you have already learned and use this knowledge to best help your child.

I found it quite a change to help Robin learn to read after working with Josh and Noah. Robin was not upset if I corrected him. Of course, having worked with his older brothers I asked him if it was OK with him if I corrected him before we started. That probably would have made it easier right from the start with Josh. Robin and I could work together without as much effort on my part. Part of that was who Robin was as well as who I had become after the experience of working with his brothers. Holly, too, has benefited from my greater experience.

Your attitude toward homeschooling is another vital component to assess when you find yourself overwhelmed and burned out. It's important that you do the things you do as a homeschooling mother because you have chosen them based on your values, your commitment, and your philosophy of homeschooling. If you feel that you must do things for other people's reasons, you will not be able to survive. It's OK to find someone to tutor your child in math, science, English, or whatever if they have a passion for a particular subject that you are not knowledgable about. If you feel that you must do everything, then soon you'll lose the ability to enjoy your child. Homeschooling then becomes drudgery. It's vital to reassess if this begins to happen.

Another component of preventing burnout is setting priorities. Just why am I homeschooling? What is it that I am trying to accomplish? With the answers to these questions, we can look at the activities that engage us and sort them out in order of priority. It's easy to get caught up in a whirlwind of activity and find yourself continuing things that are no longer of value just because you've done them before.

It can be helpful for the whole family to take time to sit and talk together about the activities everyone participates in and the reason for those activities. It can help family members have a new appreciation for each other during intense times - such as end of the year dance recitals.

When I had three boys playing baseball, I asked for help with some of the daily kitchen chores because I was overwhelmed. My boys could see that I needed the help, and we worked out a schedule. Taking time to discuss things as a family helps all members of the family work together better.

Family discussion helps children to understand why they need to help out at certain times more than others. It can also help everyone in the family learn about what motivates different family members to do what they do. Learning to take time to assess one's motivation for doing something is a helpful lifelong skill. This leads into the next topic to help prevent burnout: reevaluating one's activities and commitments.

As I mentioned in the chapter about curriculum, it's OK to stop doing something that you have started to do. It is not one of life's rules that you must finish an activity once you've started it.

One of the favorite comments elementary teachers made on re-port cards when I was young was "so and so does not finish the tasks he was assigned to do." We forget that when we homeschool, we set the agenda. If we decide half way through that this is not the way we want to keep going, it is only sensible to stop.

My boys played baseball for about three years. For Noah, baseball was a very important activity. After the baseball season was over the year that he was 13, Noah worked very hard to build strength in his arm and shoulder muscles so that he would be an even better pitcher. One month before the start of baseball season and just before Noah turned 14, he was diagnosed with Type I Diabetes. He lost many pounds and all the muscles he had worked so hard to develop. Two weeks after he came home from the hos-pital, he attended baseball tryouts. After the tryouts, he decided that baseball wasn't worth the hassle it would involve arranging his schedule of meals and insulin injections to coincide with the games. The hassle did not balance out the fun of playing baseball. I was surprised by his decision as baseball had been so important to him.

Robin made a decision to stop playing baseball after play-ing on a 10 year old tournament team. He found that although he enjoyed playing, he was distressed by the expectations one of the coaches had for his son. Robin decided that baseball wasn't fun enough to be worth the distress he felt watching adults hassle their children. This was not an easy decision for him as he had some very mixed feelings.

When I find myself reading the end of a book to see how it resolves, I realize that either I am bored by the book and I stop reading it, or I am not sure I will agree with the ending. Rather than spend my time reading the whole thing, I read the end first. It cer-tainly surprises me to find myself doing this. I was sure that I had to read a book from start to finish once I started it. I can see how silly this idea is - it is a reader's choice after all to read a book in whatever order or sequence that appeals. It may make more sense to start at the beginning and read to the end, but there is no law written anywhere that says that this is the way it must be done. And if there were, how could it be enforced? Picturing a book police force in my mind, checking all the readers of the world helps me to laugh about other things I think I must do in a certain order or from start to finish. It helps me to remember that I am in charge.

At the same time that it is important to change when an activity or project no longer suits us, we need to consider the other people who may be involved when we change. Robin continued until the end of the tournament season, but he didn't want to play anymore after that. He can remember how glad he was that the team didn't win their tournament and go on to play more games. At the same time, he played his best because he wanted to feel good about his playing and was sad when his team lost. Accepting that we can have both positive and negative feelings about the same event is often difficult. Finding a balance between our commitment to ourselves and our commitment to others requires time and thought. Some situations are easy to resolve. Others, such as changing the way we educate our children, take more time.

We need to give ourselves permission to change; to no longer take part in things that we thought defined us. Some families start homeschooling after years of school because children are unhappy and not learning even though parents may have made a commitment to making school work. Some children start going to school after being homeschooled because circumstances have changed even though parents were committed to homeschooling.

Families that homeschool may homeschool for the entire 12 schooling years of a child's life or for a portion thereof. Some families decide after a few years of homeschooling that their children would benefit from going to school. Others decide to homeschool after a time spent in school. There is no one "right" way.

When a choice is made to change, it may seem as though the first choice made was wrong. In the case of sending a child to school after homeschooling, you might feel as though the only way to justify making the change from homeschooling to schooling is by thinking that you were wrong to homeschool in the first place; to deny the validity of what you did at home.

I think it's important to keep in mind that homeschooling does not invalidate schooling nor does schooling invalidate homeschooling. There are many ways of meeting children's needs for education. I like to imagine that finding education suitable for a child and family is like going to a shoe store. No one would expect that every child would wear the same size or style of shoe. Feet are so individual. Our children's educational needs are individual, too.

When we make a change like changing from homeschooling to schooling, we may feel sheepish. We may feel that those who disagreed with our decision in the first place were right all along. This is difficult to face. What has helped me in situations like this is to try to see beyond black and white and see the gray areas when making a decision. Like finding shoes for one's child, finding the appropriate method of education is acknowledging change and growth. You would never expect your child to wear the same size or style of shoes at the age of 12 as he wore when he was 2 years old - his feet are different.

When you change from homeschooling to schooling or vice versa you are saying that things have changed. It could be your personal circumstances; it could be a child's request; it could be any number of things, but things have changed. It is more damaging to hold on to an idea that will no longer work for either you or your child or deny that a change in your circumstances, attitude, or ability has happened than to change. Your method of schooling your child at one time fit your circumstances as best as you could determine. Now, the foot has grown and it must be fit with a new shoe.

Sometimes that means a big change - homeschooling to school or vice versa - or it could be a small change - trying a new method of homeschooling such as correspondence courses or "unschooling" when you have been following a set curriculum of studies.

If you make a change, be honest and clear to your child about the reasons. If there is no choice, then do not expect that the reasons you give your child will make the change easier. He or she may be experiencing a lot of different feelings from rage to relief. However, if you are honest with your child about the reasons, and word those reasons so that no blame is attached to the child (in other words, you own responsibility for the change) then at least your child knows where he stands. In some cases, it's a child who initiates the change from homeschooling to school or the other way around and it may be the parent who needs time to adjust.

If a child initiates the desire for change remember what I wrote about in the previous chapter regarding taking responsibility for age appropriate decisions. I, personally, would have a very difficult time letting a child under the age of 12 or 13 make a decision to go to school. It seems to me that a child of younger than 12 or 13 does not have enough information or life-experience to make such a decision.

If this kind of change happens in your family, give yourself time to adjust. It takes at least 6 months to accommodate a major life-style change. Major change is not easy. It requires a willingness to trust in the process of life and growth. We can often accept change that takes place within a certain framework, i.e., we expect our children to change from crawling babies to 10 year olds who can ride bikes, but we often barricade ourselves from change that goes beyond our framework of how life is supposed to be, i.e., a child who likes school after having been homeschooled. It's uncomfortable because it is discontinuous change rather than just an incremental change.

The same discomfort may exists when a child is home-schooled after being in school. It is an unexpected change that takes time to fit into our world view.

When children become learners at home instead of going to school, it may take quite a while before everyone is comfortable with the change. At first, a child may be happy to no longer have the pressure of school, then boredom may set in. It may be tempting to decide that "Augh!! This isn't working!" especially when a child is frustrated and complains about things. Give it time. Both you and your child need to learn new ways of being together, new expectations of each other, and how to work together.

The same applies if you are changing from homeschooling to having your children in school. You may doubt the wisdom of your decision, especially if your children express unhappiness. You may also doubt all that you did at home, if your child likes school. It will take time for all of you to adjust to this new pattern in your lives. Give it time.

I hope that what I have written helps you to have the courage to listen to your heart about meeting your children's educational needs and to make changes if they are needed. While I chose to homeschool my children for all of their K-12 schooling years, I know that not all mothers who choose to homeschool will choose to homeschool for as long as I have or in the ways that I have. That, I see is one of the strengths of homeschooling - it's variety and flexibility.

Moving back to burnout, one thing that I've found very important to prevent burnout is developing a life of my own. Home-schooling doesn't mean you must devote every moment of your life to your children. "Yes," I can hear you say, "but how do I find the time?" I wish I could give you an easy to follow recipe but there isn't one.

The following are some suggestions that have worked for

some women. Before trying any of them, take time to look at the inner conflict that you may find when you take time for yourself. We carry around so many images of what it means to be a woman, a mother, a homeschooling mother. They are often in opposition to what it means to be a woman who has her own life.

My volunteer work with La Leche League gave me a place to use my talents while not taking me physically away from my children. Not very many organizations recognize that while it's important for a mother to have a life of her own, it is also vital that she not give up her life as a mother to have that life of her own. My volunteer work as a La Leche League Leader meant I could lead discussion groups with my babies and small children present, stopping to tend to their needs as necessary. As my children grew older and weren't happy attending meetings, I switched jobs. I did a job that involved a lot of correspondence. I could write or read my mail as I sat at the playground while my children played or as I sat in the stands while they participated in sports activities.

Mothers have just as great a need to be with their babies and toddlers as those babies and toddlers have a need to be with their mothers. We were meant to form attachments to our children. It is only while actually taking care of and mothering our babies and toddlers that we learn how to mother.

Our society has a difficult time with attachment. As a culture, we are so terribly afraid of intimacy that we place an inordinate value on independence in young children. We belittle the attachment of children to their mothers with phrases like "Mama's boy," "tied to her apron strings," etc. We encourage mothers to find their own lives away from their children. Never imagining or realizing until it is too late that when we encourage mothers in this way, we encourage mothers to distance themselves from their children and thereby deny a vital part of themselves. (This topic - the importance and value of mothering for a woman who is a mother -

is beyond the scope of this book. It's a subject that passionately interests me and its the basis of a book that I've been working on for many years.)

Let's look at some of the ways to develop our lives that don't require separation from our children. Reading, both to myself and aloud to my children, helped me to take mini-vacations each day. Good books gave me a chance to view the world from another perspective. Reading allowed me to enter a different space and kept me sane. Even with four small children, I always found time to read to myself. It was absolutely vital for my survival.

Some women I know enjoy doing needlework. They say it gives them a sense of peace and relaxation that helps them to slow down after a day of meeting children's needs. Others write in journals or online to satisfy their need for time to themselves. Some women find that running or going for a walk can also give them a lift. A kitchen timer is a helpful tool here. Set the timer before going out the door to help your child know when you will be back and make sure you return at that time. (This assumes that there is an adult or teenager available to take care of younger children.)

Some women use the time that they are waiting while their children attend a class to do needle work, knit, read, write in journals, etc. It's uninterrupted time - you don't have to answer the phone. If you have more than one child and one child is with you while the other is attending a class, you could use this time as a special time with this child - reading, playing card games, talking or going for a walk.

Another important part of preventing burnout is to have a support system as I mentioned in the first chapter. You may find that your support system changes as your needs change. That's only to be expected. At one time in your life, it may be very important to be in touch with other homeschooling women. At other times, you may find that you have no interest in this. Like those imaginary book police checking up to see if everyone is reading a book from start to finish, there is no one out there dictating to you how to find your support.

Overload is a common characteristic shared by all mothers. I hope that my suggestion that you develop your own life doesn't cause you more stress and conflict. I don't want to create the impression that as well as homeschooling your children, you should become a writer, an artist, an embroidery specialist, a marathon runner, or anything else. Homeschooling itself will be one way of developing your life. My intent in this chapter was to give you some ideas for preventing burnout, not to cause it.

Tension releasers

1. Go outside. Being in the natural world often calms young and old alike. Going to the beach has been one of my favorite ways to restore myself. Hearing the birds and the sound of the waves as

they reach the shore, seeing the light on the water, the flotsam and jetsam on the beach, my children playing in the sand and the large expanse of water helped me to breathe more deeply. When I was at the beach, I felt in touch with something bigger than myself. It gave me perspective.

2. Make sure that everyone has had something to eat or drink recently, including yourself.

3. Engage in some sort of physical activity - dancing in the living room, running outside, skipping rope, stretching, yoga, playing soccer, baseball, basketball, croquet, etc.

4. Blow bubbles.

5. Hang a spoon from your nose.

6. Take time to meditate, pray or visualize. I did this in the morning while I showered instead of in the evening because I tended to fall asleep then. Doing some sort of visualization, meditation while I shower helps me stay grounded during the day.

My favorite is a shortened version taken from the book *Ask Your Angels* by Alma Daniel, Timothy Wyllie, and Andrew Ramer. I imagine roots coming out of the bottom of my feet and legs going into the ground, through the floor of the shower, the room below until the roots reach into the earth beneath my house and then down into the center of the earth. I then breath the energy of the earth up through my roots and into my heart. As I exhale, I send that energy pumping through my blood stream from my heart. I do this for three or four breaths and then imagine long filaments, like branches, reaching up from the top of my head and shoulders out past the roof and through the atmosphere to the stars. I then breath the energy of the stars into my heart and exhale that energy through my blood stream from my heart for three or four breaths. Then, I imagine energy coming from both the center of the earth and the stars into my heart and being pumped around by my heart. I find this exercise helps me to be centered. If I still have time and feel like it, I then surround myself with pink roses, below, above, beside, in front of and behind me before I open my eyes and finish showering.

When I forget to meditate for too long, I begin to lose touch with myself. Now that my children are adults, I have time to meditate. However it's not built into my day as it was when they were young. The quiet times when I breastfed my babies and toddlers were the beginning of my regular meditation times. There is something very soothing for mom and babe alike when breastfeeding. I found it centered and calmed me. (That wonderful hormone prolactin!) Meditating has the same effect but I have to remember to do it. When I had a nursing baby, the baby would remind me.

7. Don't "should" on your self! Let go of those preconceived notions that a mother should ...always be patient ...have fresh cookies available ...have all the laundry sorted and folded as soon as it's

washed ...provide an interesting and challenging learning atmosphere all the time ...answer all the questions that children ask. Choose activities for your own reasons. Let go of the guilt of the "shoulds."

7. Get enough sleep! (Is this a should?)

8.. Take time to enjoy your children! Look them in the eye and see the love that you share.

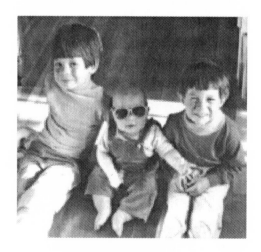

Josh, Robin, and Noah

Here's a quote I saw on the desk of a church secretary when I was booking space for a concert:
Do not feel totally, ultimately, and completely responsible for everything.
   That's my job!
   Thanks, God

And an old Scottish saying:

Angels fly because they take themselves lightly!

Holly

Heron Rocks, Hornby Islandn, BC

CHAPTER 9
Beyond Homeschooling

No book on homeschooling would be complete without looking at what happens after homeschooling. Can someone who homeschools go to college or university? get a job? succeed in life? Yes. Homeschooling will not jeopardize your child's chances of finding work nor will it jeopardize his or her acceptance to an institution of higher learning. Your child may need to do some extra work to demonstrate aptitude, ability and competency, but homeschooling does not close doors to jobs or further education. In fact, from what I've observed, young people who have been homeschooled have a sense of self-confidence and poise that will help them in any field they choose to pursue.

The concerns you have about higher education or job possibilities when you have a 6 year old are going to be different than the concerns you will have when that child is 16 years old. Over the subsequent years of homeschooling, your child will develop interests and abilities.   Children of today may have as many as five different careers over their lifetime. The different interests homebased learners have had the opportunity to pursue will stand them in good stead to be able to adapt to the changing world of work. The experience homebased learners have in setting their own schedules, designing their own days will also be of great benefit when they are adults.

If your child is interested in attending a college or university and shows proficiency in reading, writing, and the ability to do math, then entrance to post-secondary education institutions can be achieved. Things are changing all the time. More and more post-secondary institutions recognize homebased learners as motivated learners. Rather than give you specifics on how to go about finding post secondary schools that will accept homebased learners, I suggest you search the internet for up-to-date information about this.   Here are two sites:

A-Z Home's Cool

homeschooling.gomilpitas.com/olderkids/Admission.htm

Canadian information try:

www.ontariohomeschool.org/universityCanada.shtml/

By the time your read this book, these sites may no longer exist. If you type in college/university and homeschooling, you'll find a number of links that will provide you with helpful information.

Some people get a GED instead of a traditional high school diploma. I was curious about the General Education Diploma (GED) tests when my oldest were in their teens. I borrowed a book from the library about how to prepare to take a GED. The sample tests were all multiple choice. I wanted my children to know how to take multiple choice tests so I used these tests as a learning tool. We discovered that what was most important when taking these tests was knowing how to read for information and how to think critically. Even though some of the material in the tests was not familiar, the tests had enough explanatory information to make it possible to answer the questions - comprehension and critical thinking. My children found these tests easy to do. Even the youngest members of the family, who were between 7-11 at the time, could answer many of the questions.

The Scholastic Aptitude Test (SAT) or a similar test such as the National Merit Scholarship Qualifying Test (NMSQT) are a different matter. Many institutions use the scores of these tests as a gage of a student's aptitude for college level work. The SAT does not have the same kind of explanatory material as the high school equivalency test because it tests for verbal and mathematical aptitude rather than comprehension. SAT preparation tests are available online or in books from your library.

SAT tests can help you establish a homeschooled child's aptitude to do college/university level work. Keep in mind that these tests have a certain bias. See the book *None of the Above: Behind the Myth of Scholastic Aptitude* by David Owen for an in depth look at the SAT.

Most high schools in the U.S. and some in Canada offer the SAT test in both the fall and spring to their grade 11 and 12 students. If you are interested in having your child take this test, check with your local public and/or private high school to find out how your child can take this test. You can also go the website *collegeboard.com* to find upcoming test locations. If your child decides to take an SAT test, help him/her by setting up practice test situations with time periods and old SAT tests. The college board site has a number of practice questions that you can try and explanations of what they are looking for in answers. The experience gained from these practice sessions will make it easier to take the actual test.

Keep in mind as you explore the possibilities of higher education that acquiring information is no longer tied to a specific location. As I mentioned in chapter 7, computer technology has changed our lives in ways that we have yet to acknowledge. Your child can use this technology to acquire post-secondary degrees. Just as you have educated your child in a nontraditional way by helping your child to learn at home, you and your child can explore various options for college or university. It doesn't have to be four years spent in one location, going to classes, and then graduating, although some students do choose to do this. Just be aware that there are distance diploma mills that offer degrees but are not accredited schools.

Something else to consider is early admittance to community college programs. Some community colleges will take students in their early teens as long as they have passed certain entrance requirements. Keep in mind that earlier doesn't necessarily mean better.

Those who go on to college or university after learning at home may find it a challenge at first. For some students the pace in college or university courses may be too slow and tedious, for others it may look confusing, especially if very little formal studying has been done previously. It may be helpful to encourage your college student to take less than a full course load at first. Your support and encouragement during this time in your child's life is just as vital as before.

Trade and technical schools can be approached in the same way as colleges or universities. Find out what kind of documentation they need to admit a homeschooled student. Ask if they are flexible in their requirements for admission.

Not every homeschooling child will want or need to go to college or university. One of the important things to do during the later teen years is to encourage your teenager to discover just what fields interest him or her. You can then explore together what sort of work is available in those fields and how to go about entering those fields.

One homeschooler that I knew wanted to do something in the field of dance. She asked each of her dance teachers - ballet, folk, Hawaiian, tap, jazz, and flamingo - what the possibility was for her to become a professional dancer in that field. She then asked each of them what other possibilities there were if she could not be a professional dancer. Each of her teachers responded with a lot of information. One teacher told her about the field of dance notation - a field that needs more people. This opened up a field of study that she hadn't known about before.

When a homeschooled young adult applies for a job, it is just as important to document ability, competency, special interests or talents as it is for entrance to college, university, or a technical program. What is most important to any employer is whether or not the person applying for the job can do the work and is reliable enough to do the work. Documents that demonstrate reliability and responsibility are valuable references. Be resourceful when writing a résumé. Use experiences, a portfolio, an audio or video tape to demonstrate competency, ability, and willingness to learn new skills.

I hope this gives you a glimpse into the possibilities after homeschooling. Once a person is beyond the traditional schooling years, schooling methods are not as important as aptitude, ability, and commitment. If you have helped your children master the basics of reading, writing, and arithmetic, then they will be able to acquire other skills as needed.

Homeschooling can lead your family in directions you never expected. When children learn in nontraditional ways, they can also think in nontraditional ways. A number of people have com-

mented to me how struck they have been by my children's original-
ity and creative thinking abilities: "each child is unique, not one is a
cookie cutter version of the other."

I think the world can use as many creative and original think-
ers as possible. People who can see around what has always been
done to find new ways to do things are in short supply. I think of
my friend's homeschooled son, who was enrolled in a co-op computer engineering program at a university. During one of his work
terms, he read through the waiver he was being asked to sign, and
said he wouldn't sign it. The waiver not only waived ownership of
work done for the company, but also past and future work that
might be done on one's own. The boss asked him why he wouldn't
sign, so he explained. The form was redesigned.

This young man also noticed that some of the work that
people needed to do was not being done very efficiently, and asked
if he could do some reprogramming to fix this. He told his boss
that he had extra time and it wouldn't interfere with his own work.
He was given permission and went ahead and fixed it. Throughout
the next day, various workers came to the boss and asked what
happened - work that used to take them 45 minutes to do, now
only took 10 minutes. The boss explained. The boss offered this
young man a full time position as soon as he graduated.

Not every child who homeschools will be a computer genius. However, when children are learning at home in non-regi-
mented ways, they have the opportunity to observe and draw conclusions on their own, often leading to creative and original thinking. I once read "stupidity" defined as "continuing to do the same
things in the same way and expecting a different outcome." My
brother pointed out to me after reading the first edition of this
book that if you reverse the thinking of this statement, it is the
scientific method - "doing something in the same way should have
the same outcome."

New ways of thinking and new ways of looking at things are desperately needed. Children who have had the opportunity to think for themselves, to discover and explore the world at their own pace may grow up to be adults who are able to find new insights into old problems. I was astonished by the astute observations that my children made when they were young and continue to be so now that they are adults.

Let me give you an example. I described an incident from a book I was reading, *Raising Cain: Protecting the Emotional Life of Boys* by Dan Kindlon, Ph.D. and Michael Thompson, Ph.D., to one of my children. The incident involved a boy who had punched a hole in the wall of his bedroom. His mother sent him to the school psychologist (one of the authors) because she couldn't figure out what was making her son so angry. The psychologist eventually got the boy to talk. It turned out he wasn't angry, he was sad. It took a lot of work on the part of the psychologist before the boy trusted him enough to open up and share his sadness.

My child who was about 12 at the time made the following comments. "Anger gets results. Sadness doesn't. When this boy was a baby, probably his parents didn't respond to his nighttime crying. So he learned that when he was sad, nobody paid any attention. Parents teach their children that sad doesn't get a response. Anger, smashing walls, is different - it gets a response."

What an insightful observation! The authors of this book took many pages to say basically the same thing - how important it is to be responsive to your children, to give them reason to trust you by listening to them and to demonstrate your love by your actions.

My children often made comments like these in our discussions. They offered me a fresh perspective or unexpected perceptions. The comments that my children shared with me often opened doors in my mind that I didn't even know were closed. One of the reasons I didn't want to send my children away from home for six hours a day is that I wanted to hear their observations, the conclusions they drew about what they had seen, read, or heard. This was one of the best parts of homeschooling for me.

In closing, let me state again that homeschooling is not a panacea that will cure any or all of the ills of education. Deciding to homeschool is a commitment to a process of education that takes a tremendous amount of time and effort. It requires an alertness and awareness that can at times be draining, yet those who have done it find that the work involved is more than balanced by the rewards.

Two women whose children are adults in their 20s and 30s talked to me about the benefits of homeschooling.

The closeness of my relationship to my children. My daughter and I are much closer than I was to my mother at her age. My daughter and I have shared so much together.

I've grown up with my children. I was there while they were growing up so that I know them. Some women I know seem to be afraid of their older children. They don't know who they are. By making an unusual choice in educating my children, by 'bucking the system,' I have gained confidence to pursue ideas or ways of doing things that are unusual in other fields

I worked hard to help my children reach their potential, so in the process I had to discover my own. In order for me to help them reach their potential, I had to model reaching for mine. I am doing things now that I never imagined I would be doing in the world of fashion. I never thought I would win a trip to Paris!

By being at home and homeschooling my children, I was myself. If my children had gone to school, I would have gone back to work as a teacher. I would never have belonged to myself.

I still get butterflies in my stomach when I think about how exciting it (homeschooling) is even now.

Being a homeschooling mother requires a commitment to your children and yourself to create a learning environment that is safe as well as stimulating. It requires a commitment to take the time and make the effort to nurture and support your children as they grow. It means building a caring and intimate relationship with your child. It will require all that you have to give and more. And yet, what else would you want to give?

Your life may change in ways that you do not expect: I never imagined I would perform as a children's entertainer in a shopping mall to help make payments on the loan for Josh's harp. I never imagined I would write a book about homeschooling, although writing has always been of interest to me. Not only have my children done things that delight and surprise me, I have delighted myself by the skills I developed and strengthened as I helped my children learn at home.

If you enjoy your child and have "butterflies" of excitement thinking about how much you'd like to try homeschooling, then do it. You and your child are about to start on an exciting adventure!

Acknowledgments and Notes

Thanks to the many readers who took the time to write to me to over the years to tell me that my book helped them feel confident enough to homeschool and to all of those who have attended the workshops and presentations I've done over the years. Your spontaneous positive feedback continues to amaze me. Many thanks to my family for their ongoing support and encouragement.

APPENDIX I
Read Aloud Books Not Mentioned Elsewhere

Burch, Robert: *Ida Early Comes Over The Mountain; Christmas With Ida Early* 6-8 and up

Godden, Rumer: *Didokai* for ages 9 and up; *Holly and Ivy* 4 and up; *Home is the Sailor* f 6-7 and up; other books by this author

Erickson, Russell E.: *Warton and Morton; A Toad For Tuesday; Warton and The Castaways; Warton and The Contest; Warton and The King Of The Skies; Warton's Christmas Eve Adventure* 4 and up

Goodall, Jane: *My Life With The Chimpanzees* 10-12 and up

King-Smith, Dick: *Harry's Mad, The Cuckoo Child, Sheep Pig, Pigs Might Fly* and others 5 and up

Lewis, C.S.: The *Lion, The Witch, and The Wardrobe*, etc. 6-7 and up

Lindgren, Astrid: *The Brothers' Lionheart* 7-8 and up

Paulsen, Gary: *Hatchet* and other books 11-12 and up

Trease, Geoffrey: *Bows Against The Barons* 8-9 and up; *Cue For Treason* 9-10 and up; and other books

APPENDIX II
Make a Rope Ladder

You may wish to increase the dimensions of both the length of the dowel and the length of the rope between each dowel depending on the size of your child. These instructions will suit a child up to about age 7-9 years old.

<u>Supplies needed:</u>

2   1" diameter x 3' long dowel rods cut to 1 foot lengths

16' of ¼" nylon braid

1. Drill 1/4" holes one inch from the ends of the one foot dowel pieces.

2. Thread rope through holes in the first dowel, putting the middle of the rope in the middle of the dowel.

3. Tie knots in the rope over each hole.

4. Tie a knot 12" up on each side of the rope.

5. Thread each end of the rope through the next dowel rod, and tie a knot above the hole. Make sure the knot is bigger than the hole so that the rope does not slip through.

6. Continue in this manner, tying a knot 12" up on each side until all the dowel rods have been secured.

7. Hang with screw eyes or tie around a branch. Move knots around to level dowel rods.

8. Test ladder with adult weight for security before allowing a child to climb or swing on it

APPENDIX III
Goal Setting

1. **Current Activities:** List what you (or your family) are doing now – include all activities such as purchasing food, clothes, etc., cleaning house, reading stories, etc. If you are working with others, share your lists and add to your own if appropriate. Set these aside, temporarily. (3 min.)

2. **Needs/Wants:** Quietly, individually, reflect on your (or your family's) needs or wants. Visualize the perfect situation and what you need to create that situation. (1 min.)

3. **Sharing Needs/Wants:** List – on a flip chart, blackboard, or large piece of paper – the needs/wants that you and/or each person in the group has visualized. (5 min.)

4. **Choosing Goals:** You have three stars (if you are working in a group, each person has three stars) to use to vote for what needs or wants are most important. You can put all three in one place, one on each of three different places, or however you want to use your three stars. After everyone has voted with their stars, pick the three needs with the most stars. From these choose one. This now becomes your goal. (2-5 min.)

5. **Writing And Sharing An Objective Goal Statement:** Write a statement about the goal you have just selected that tells exactly what you want to accomplish. Be as specific as possible (include numbers, dates, etc.) so that you can measure or observe your progress toward achieving your goal. If you are working with someone else, share this statement with them. Here's an example. Let's say that you have as your goal to be more patient because you are not happy that you are losing your temper 4 or more times a day. An objective statement would be - I will increase my patience by 25% by the end of 60 days. I will not lose my temper more than three times a day. (5-10 min.)

6. **Brainstorming Possibilities:** List all ideas that can help you achieve your goal. Remember, when you are brainstorming – any idea is valid no matter how unlikely, impossible, or silly it may seem. Record without judgment. (5-10 Min.)
Using the example, here's a list of brainstorming ideas about   increasing one's patience:

   1. Get a patience transplant
   2. Have hired help
   3. Take a nap everyday
   4. Have your children take naps every day
   5. Have Mary Poppins come and entertain your children twice a week
   6. Learn hypnotism, so that you can hypnotize yourself to be more patient
   7. Hypnotize your children so that they do not do things that call

on your patience

8. Purchase a tank of nitrous oxide, laughing gas, to use when you are on the edge

9. Reduce the number of activities family members participate in

7. **Action Steps:** Using the brainstorming list in combination with the first list that you made (current activities), pick out those items that will be most effective in accomplishing your goal. Under the items that you choose, list specific steps that you will take.

Using the example: If you have listed that you have too much house work and run out of patience when your children want you to read a story, you might consider getting a neighborhood teenager to come and read stories to your children while you do a housecleaning blitz. Or you may decide to hire a neighborhood teenager to clean the bathroom and do a number of loads of laundry while you read to your children. You may not be able to afford full time help, but you can find ways to lessen your burden. Sometimes, women get together and share housework, while one mother reads or plays games with all the children.

8. **Time Table:** Working backwards from your target date or perhaps an event, build a time table for the action steps you have listed. This is more useful as a step in goal setting when you have a specific event or goal you want to accomplish such as planning a birthday party or another celebration. For more general life style changes, a time table may cause stress. The intention of goal setting is to relieve stress. Don't let the time table or your action steps get in the way of enjoying your life.

Using the example, you may decide that in a month's time after using the new approaches you have outlined, you will reassess the goals you set and the ways in which you implemented those goals.

9. **Assignments:** Decide for each step in the action plan who will do what by when. This is a very critical part when planning with a group or more than one person. It is important for each person to know who is going to do what when, in order to implement any changes. This is also a time to set up when the action plan will be reviewed.

This goal setting and action planning method can be used to help children decide what they want to do by modifying the technique so that it is appropriate for their age. You could ask children to draw a picture on a card that describes the activities that they want to do —a different card for each activity. Then you can look at those cards together and ask your child to put them in order of what they most want to do to least want to do (priorize them). You can then discuss why these activities are important. From there you can brainstorm how to accomplish these goals.

Bibliography

Chapter 1:
1. *How Children Learn; How Children Fail* by John Holt
2. *De-schooling Society* by Ivan Illich
3. *Your Child's Growing Mind* by Jane M. Healy, Ph.D.
4. *People Skills* by Robert Bolton
5. *How To Talk So Kids Will Listen And Listen So Kids Will Talk* by Faber and Mazlish
6. *Mastering Your Hidden Self* by Serge King
7. Books by Alice Miller - *For Your Own Good*, etc.
9. *Discipline: Kids Are Worth It* by Barbara Coloroso
10. *No Contest: The Case Against Competition* by Alfie Kohn
11. *Teach Only Love* by Gerald Jampolsky, M.D.

Chapter 2:
1. *How Tom Beat Captain Najork And His Hired Sportsmen* by Russell Hoban
2. *Truckers* by Terry Pratchett
3. *Women Who Run With The Wolves* by Clarisa Pinkola Estes
4. Books by Alice Miller
5. *How To Parent* by Fitzhugh Dodson
6. *How Children Learn* by John Holt
7. *How To Really Love Your Child* by Ross Campbell
8. *The World of Lego Toys* by Henry Wiencek
9. *Noah's Ark* by Rien Poortvliet

Chapter 3:
1. *Teacher* by Sylvia Ashton Warner
2. *The Read-Aloud Handbook* by Jim Trelease
3. *The Honey Hunt; The Bears' Christmas* by Jan and Stan Berenstain
4. *More Spaghetti, I Say!* by Rita Gelman
5. *Charlotte's Web; The Trumpet of The Swan* by E.B. White
6. *Aha! Insight* by Martin Gardner
7. *The Art of Education* by Rudolph Steiner
8. *How Children Learn*, etc. by John Holt
9. *A Farmer's Alphabet* by Mary Azarian
10. Little Bear books by Else Minarik
11. *Oliver And Amanda's Christmas* by Jan Van Leeuwen
12. All the Frog and Toad books and *Owl At Home* by Arnold Lobel

13. *Nate the Great and the ...* by Marjorie Weinman Sharmat
14. *Why Johnny Can't Read; Why Johnny Still Can't Read* by Rudolph Flesch
15. *Games for Reading* by Peggy Kaye
16. *The Lives of Children* by George Dennison
17. *The Sounds of...* Readers by Bill Martin, Jr.
18. *Teaching the Universe of Discourse* by James Moffett

Chapter 4:
1. *Grooks* by Piet Hein
2. *Brain Sex: The Real Difference Between Men and Women* by Anne Moire, Ph.D. and David Jessel
3. *The Female Brain* by Louann Md Brizendine
4. *Men Are From Mars, Women Are From Venus* by John Gray, Ph.D.
5. *Learning All the Time* by John Holt
6. *English Grammar and Composition* by John E. Warriner
7. *The Elements of Style* by William Strunk, Jr. and E.B. White
8. *How To Write Plain English* by Rudolph Flesch

Chapter 5:
1. *How Children Fail* by John Holt
2. http://en.wikipedia.org/wiki/Martin_Gardner
3. http://en.wikipedia.org/wiki/Raymond_Smullyan
4. *Mathematics, A Human Endeavor; Geometry; Algebra* by Harold Jacobs
5. http://en.wikipedia.org/wiki/Jean_Piaget
6. *Origami Made Easy; Creative Origami* by Kunihiko Kasahara
7. *Origami* by Paulo Mulatinho
8. *Classic Origami* by Paul Jackson
9. *The World of Origami* by Isao Honda
10. *Teachers and Machines: The Classroom Use of Technology Since 1920* (1986) by Larry Cuban
11. *Silicon Snake Oil: Second Thoughts on the Information Highway* (1995) by Clifford Stoll
12. *Endangered Minds: Why Children Can't Think and What We Can Do About It* (1990) by Jane Healy
13. *The End of Education* (1995) by Neil Postman
14. *Life On Screen: Identity in the Age of the Internet* (1995) by Sherry Turkle
15. *The Flickering Mind -Saving Education from the False Promise of Technology* by Todd Oppenheimer
16. http://l3d.cs.colorado.edu/philosophy.html#1.4

Chapter 6

1. *Superlearning* by S. Ostrander and L. Schroeder
2. *Drawing on the Right Side of the Brain* by Betty Edwards
3. *Great Painters* by Piero Ventura
4. *Teddybears and How To Make Them* by Margaret Hutchings
5. *How To Raise A Healthy Child In Spite of Your Doctor* by Robert Mendelsohn, M.D.
6. *Homeopathic Medicine At Home* by Maesimand Panos, M. D. and Jane Heimlich
7. *The Plug-In Drug* by Marie Winn
8. *Lives of Musicians* by Kathleen Krull
9. *Bill Peet: An Autobiography* by Bill Peet
10. *Beethoven Lives Upstairs* by Classical Kids recordings
11. Storytellers:
    a. Jay O'Callahan www.ocallahan.com
    b. Doug Lipman www.storydynamics.com
    c. Danny Kaye
    d. National Storytellers Association www.storytellingfoundation.org

Chapter 7

1. *If You Want To Be Rich and Happy, Don't Go To School* by Robert T. Kiyosaki
2. *Bingo Long and the Travelling All Stars* (film) book by William Brashler
3. *Misty of Chincoteague; Sea Star; Stormy; Misty's Foal* by Marguerite Henry
4. *Sheep Pig; Pigs Might Fly; Harry's Mad* and others by Dick King-Smith
5. *Bet You Can; Bet Can't* by Vicki Cobb
6. The Magic School Bus series by Joanna Cole
7. "The Wheel of the Water" song by Tom Chapin from *Mother Earth*
8. Eyewitness Jr. series published by Alfred Knopf
9. *Benny's Animals* by Millicent E. Selsam
10. *Richard Scarry's What Do People Do All Day; Great Big Air Book*
11. *Huck Scarry's Things That Fly; Things That Go*
12. *How we are BORN How we GROW How our bodies WORK and How we LEARN* by Joe Kaufman
13. *My Family and Other Animals* and other books by Gerald Durrell
14. *Absolute Zero Gravity* by Betsy Devine and Joel E. Cohen
15. *Surely Your Joking, Mr. Feynman!; What Do You Care What Other People Think* by Richard Feynman
16. *The Call of Stories* by Robert Coles
17. *Margaret By Herself; Margaret In The Middle; Margaret On Her Way* by Beatrice

Hunter
18. *Cheaper by the Dozen; Belles on Their Toes* by Frank B. Gilbreth, Jr. and Ernestine Gilbreth Carey
19. *The Little House Books* by Laura Ingalls Wilder
20. The Rocky Ridge Years - *The Little House on Rocky Ridge; Little Farm in the Ozarks; In the Land of the Big Red Apple; On the Other Side of the Hill* by Roger McBride continues the Laura Ingalls Wilder books
21. *Anastatia Krupnik; Number the Stars* by Lois Lowry
22. *The Silver Sword* by Ian Serraillier
23. *The Good Master; The Singing Tree; The Chestry Oak* by Kate Seredy
24. *The House of Sixty Fathers* by Meindert de Jong
25. *Homecoming; Dicey's Song; Solitary Blue; Jackaroo* and other books by Cynthia Voigt
26. *Castle; City; Pyramid; Cathedral* by David Macaulay
27. *The Day the Universe Changed* by James Burke (both book and film series)
28. *The Living Planet* by David Attenborough Video-film series and book

Chapter 8
1. *People Skills* by Robert Bolton
2. *The Win-Win Negotiator* by Ross R. Reck, Ph.D. and Brian G. Long, Ph.D.
3. *Dance of Anger; Dance of Intimacy* Harriet Lerner
4. *Ask Your Angels* by Alma Daniels, Timothy Wyllie, Andrew Ramer
5. *Emmanuel's Book* compiled by Pat Rodegast and Judith Stanton

Chapter 9
1. *Homeschooling For Excellence* by David and Micki Colfax
2. *And What About College? How Homeschooling Can Lead To Admission To The Best Colleges and Universities* by Cafi Cohen
3. *None of the Above; Behind The Myth of Scholastic Aptitude* by David Owen
5. *Raising Cain: Protecting the Emotional Life Of Boys* by Dan Kindlon, Ph.D. and Michael Thompson, Ph.D.

Printed in the United States
148294LV00001B/22/A